Lot Dudley Young
in later years

REMINISCENCES OF A SOLDIER OF THE ORPHAN BRIGADE

by
Lieut. Lot Dudley Young
Paris, Kentucky

THE CONFEDERATE
REPRINT COMPANY
☆   ☆   ☆   ☆
WWW.CONFEDERATEREPRINT.COM

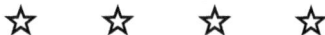

Reminiscences of a Soldier of the Orphan Brigade
by Lot Dudley Young

Originally Published in 1918
Courier-Journal Job Printing Company
Louisville, Kentucky

Reprint Edition © 2016
The Confederate Reprint Company
Post Office Box 2027
Toccoa, Georgia 30577
www.confederatereprint.com

Cover and Interior Design by
Magnolia Graphic Design
www.magnoliagraphicdesign.com

ISBN-13: 978-1945848049
ISBN-10: 1945848049

To those who wore the gray and to their children and children's children, this booklet is dedicated.

FOREWORD

☆ ☆ ☆ ☆

The Richard Hawes Chapter of the Daughters of the Confederacy warmly recommends Col. L.D. Young's *Reminiscences of the Orphan Brigade* as a most worthy addition to the literature of the South.

It is an interesting recital of the author's personal experiences and contains much valuable historic information.

The Chapter commends Mr. Young, a splendid Christian gentleman – a gallant Confederate soldier – to all lovers of history – and especially to the brave soldiers of the present great war.

THE ORPHAN BRIGADE
by Prof. N.S. Shaler
of the Federal Army

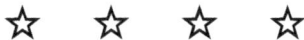

☆   ☆   ☆   ☆

Eighteen hundred and sixty-one:
There in the echo of Sumter's gun
Marches the host of the Orphan Brigade,
Lit by their banners, in hope's best arrayed.
Five thousand strong, never legion hath borne
Might as this bears it forth in that morn:
Hastings and Crecy, Naseby, Dunbar,
Cowpens and Yorktown, Thousand Years' War,
Is writ on their hearts as onward afar
They shout to the roar of their drums.

Eighteen hundred and sixty-two:
Well have they paid to the earth its due.
Close up, steady! the half are yet here
And all of the might, for the living bear
The dead in their hearts over Shiloh's field –
Rich, O God, is thy harvest's yield!
Where faith swings the sickle,
trust binds the sheaves,
To the roll of the surging drums.

Eighteen hundred and sixty-three:
Barring Sherman's march to the sea –
Shorn to a thousand; face to the foe
Back, ever back, but stubborn and slow.
Nineteen hundred wounds they take
In that service of Hell, yet the hills they shake
With the roar of their charge as onward they go
To the roar of their throbbing drums.

Eighteen hundred and sixty-four:
Their banners are tattered, and scarce twelve score,
Battered and wearied and seared and old,
Stay by the staves where the Orphans hold
Firm as a rock when the surges break –
Shield of a land where men die for His sake,
For the sake of the brothers whom they have laid low,
To the roll of their muffled drums.

Eighteen hundred and sixty-five:
The Devil is dead and the Lord is alive,
In the earth that springs where the heroes sleep,
And in love new born where the stricken weep.
That legion hath marched past the setting of sun:
Beaten? nay, victors: the realms they have won
Are the hearts of men who forever shall hear
The throb of their far-off drums.

CHAPTER ONE

☆ ☆ ☆ ☆

Kentuckians in Two Great Wars

It is for the amusement and entertainment of the thousands of young Kentuckians now enlisted beneath the Stars and Stripes in the world cataclysm of war for the cause of humanity and righteousness that these recollections and reminiscences are published. The author believing they will enable the "boys" to pass what might otherwise be at times lonesome and monotonous hours.

And while refused by the Secretary of War (by reason of age) the opportunity to participate in the great struggle now raging, it is his province now only to watch their career, to pray for them and their success, for their successful and triumphant return.

And by reason of his experience as a soldier he can enter into fully their aspirations and ambitions and share their hopes, rejoice in their victories and their triumphs. He understands the dread suspense of the impending conflict, the thrill and shock of battle, the victorious shout, the gloom and chagrin of defeat, the pangs of hunger and suffering from wounds and disease – for he has seen war in all its horrors.

And he knows that when the supreme moment comes that Kentucky blood will assert itself – that her traditional honor will be upheld, her renown glorified anew.

He knows that these inspirations will insure steadiness of step, strength of arm and force of stroke.

He rejoices that the ever assertive blood of the Anglo-Saxon flows through the veins of these young Kentuckians, ready at all times and under all circumstances to be dedicated to the cause of humanity and righteousness.

As will be readily seen, at the time of the writing of these chapters, there was no thought of the great war in which the world is now engulfed and it was mainly a work of pastime and personal satisfaction that they were then written and published. But the suggestion has been made that if published in suitable form for distribution and donated by friends to the Kentucky boys now in service that it might be appreciated by the boys "over there," some of whom are doubtless the sons or grandsons of those who composed this little band of "immortals" and who contributed so much to Kentucky's history in the unfortunate fratricidal conflict of almost sixty years ago. Thank God that the animosities of that unhappy period have long since been banished, and there is now but one thought, one aim, animating the hearts and minds of these sons and grandsons, viz., the overthrow of autocracy and the avenging of the outrages of the Huns – and a readjustment and regeneration of the relationship and affairs of men.

In the changed conditions that confront us today we see the history of the Commonwealth being absorbed by the Nation and almost imperceptibly blended into a Nationalized, Americanized whole.

And whatever of history the sons of the Commonwealth achieve in the great war will be accredited to the nation America, and not Kentucky. And recognizing this unification as a fixed policy of our government, the writer takes advantage of the opportunity in this little booklet (lest we forget) to individualize and compliment the magnificent record of that little band of Kentuckians, known in history as the "Orphan Brigade" and whose achievements form one of the most brilliant chapters in the history of the State and Nation. Hence the publication of this booklet. The writer does not for a moment stop to criticise the wisdom of this change (from the volunteer to the conscript system) and he hopes he may be pardoned for expressing pride in Kentucky's unexcelled past history. Henceforth it will not be what Kentucky or Ohio accomplished in war, but what the Nation, unified America, accomplished. It will now be "liberty enlightening" and leading the world.

Then let the battle rage and onward move,
Count not the cost nor falter in the breach,
God, the Great Commander,
wields the righteous wand,
And bids you His Love the tyrant teach.

When that shall have been accomplished (should the author be living) he will be tempted to exclaim in the language of old Moses when from Mt. Nebo he beheld the land of Canaan and exclaimed, "Now Lord, I am ready."

In writing these recollections and reminiscences he has aimed as much as possible to avoid aspersions, reflections and criticisms and confine himself to a personal knowledge, which, of course, was more or less limited, because of the restricted sphere of his activities and operations. But he assures the "boys" that his stories, while not classic, are substantially true. He could not afford to, at his advanced age, attempt to misrepresent or deceive, and he hopes the reader will excuse any irregularities in the order of publication in book form for, as previously stated, that was not originally contemplated.

In comparing conditions and surroundings of that day with those of the soldier of today, we find them so radically different as to be incomparable. And for this the soldier of today should be truly thankful, since in the case of these isolated Kentuckians – none of whom could communicate with friends and receive a message or word of cheer from the dear ones at home – circumstances today are so very, very different. And while you are called upon to meet and face many and more trying dangers, because of the new and more modern instruments of war, you are in many ways much better provided for than were your sires and grandsires. Now when sick or wounded you have every attention that modern skill and science can command. You have also the angelic help and ministrations of that greatest of all help and comfort, the Red Cross, and many other sources of help and aid that the soldiers of the past did not have.

So that while the dangers may be greater, the casualties more numerous, relief has multiplied proportionately. And you are today soldiers engaged in war which has the same meaning it has always had. Because of the gloom and sorrow that now enshrouds the world, it would be well if we could forget the past – for the events of today are but a portrayal of the past, a renewal of man's "inhumanity to man." But it has been so decreed by Him who "moves in a mysterious way His wonders to perform, Who plants His footsteps in the sea and rides upon the storm."

And let us hope – as many believe – that out of "much tribulation cometh great joy." If it were not for a great and wise purpose, how could it be? It is God's will and submission to His will is man's only choice.

So let your spirits as they rise and fall,
Ever cling to the Faith that Right will prevail,
That God will be with you to the end and is all in all,
And no foeman, freedom's banner shall assail.

It is at the instance of the Richard Hawes Chapter of the U.D.C. chiefly that the writer of these recollections and reminiscences has collected and published them.

If in contributing this history of experiences and recollections he shall give in any degree pleasure and furnish entertainment to the "dear Kentucky boys" over the seas he shall feel happy to have had that privilege and opportunity.

He assures them that none more sincerely, more prayerfully hopes for their safe and triumphant return. He knows that this triumph will be the grandest chapter in the world's history and that America will have played her part gloriously in the grand tragedy.

Oh! that he could be one of the actors!

Then will the dark and gloomy days of your absence hallowed by the blood of your lost comrades be made glorious by a triumphant return, the like of which the world has never before seen nor never will see again.

Then will every hilltop and mountain peak blaze with the bonfires of a glorious greeting.

Then will the dear old mother's heart thrill with joy and happiness. Then will the old father say, "Welcome! Welcome! my dear boy, I knew you would come." Then too will she who promised, watched, hoped and prayed be found seeking the opportunity to say, "I am now ready to redeem my promise."

Then will the old soldier (God permitting him to live) who dedicates these lines extend the glad hand of greeting to the noble boys of his acquaintance and say, "Well done, ye noble sons! I rejoice in your achievements, your victories, your triumphs. Welcome, thrice welcome, and again welcome, God smiles and the land is yours. Let justice and righteousness prevail now, henceforth and forever."

It is conceivable that forty or fifty years hence some of these soldier boys now participating in the great war will find themselves wandering over these fields upon which the greatest tragedies in the world's history are now being enacted, and it is in full comprehension (because of similar experiences) that the writer can extend the imaginations of the mind to that time.

It will be for him, who may be so fortunate, a glorious day, a thrilling and inspiring reminiscence. To be one of the actors in this stupendous tragedy in the history and affairs of the world; to see, to participate in and realize these grand events is to see things that have heretofore seemed impossible, or inconceivable.

But the times are full of wonders and amazements, and things are happening faster and faster day by day.

If the early history of the writer, read before

the U.D.C., contains matter that would seem more appropriate for a novel, because of its romantic character, he justifies himself by saying that "youth is full of romance" and he believes, yea he knows, that many a brave boy today feels the impulse and touch of these thoughts and suggestions – and not alone the soldier boy, but the modest, timid, retiring maiden whose heart quavered when she said good-bye.

CHAPTER TWO

☆ ☆ ☆ ☆

Entrance Into Confederate Service

An Address Delivered at Paris, Ky., June 26, 1916

Madame President, Ladies, Daughters of the Confederacy:

I have several times promised your ex-president, Mrs. Leer, that I would furnish her with a brief history of my observations and experiences as a soldier, and have so far failed; but will now, ere it is too late, try to comply with this promise.

But for the life of me I cannot see how I shall comply with this request without (seemingly at least) appearing in the role of one given to self praise or eulogy, and, modest man that I am, I hesitate; this will explain why I have been so long complying with your request, and shall constitute my apology.

The history of Kentucky Confederates was in most instances very similar and their duties likewise similar. All were imbued with the spirit of patriotism and love for the cause in which they had engaged, each determined to do whatever he could to promote and advance the cause in which he was enlisted. In this I claim to have done no more than other Kentucky soldiers who fought under the "Stars and Bars."

And yet there may be some incidents, some experiences in my history so different from others as to make them somewhat interesting by contrast, and as others have kindly furnished you with a history of their experience, you may be somewhat interested in making comparisons.

Now, so far as relates to my history as a real soldier, the beginning of that career was on the 8th of September, 1861. On the 22d of January following I was twenty years old – quite a youth you are ready to say. But I had been a soldier almost two years, being a charter member of that little band of "Sunday" soldiers – the "Flat Rock Grays" – and which constituted an integral part of what was known at that time as the Kentucky "State Guard."

This little company of citizen soldiers were in their conceit and imagination very important and consequential fellows. Invited to all the noted gatherings and public affairs of the day, dressed in gaudy and flashy uniforms and flying plumes, filled with pride and conceit, they did not know they were nursing their pride against the day of wrath. One only of two now living, I look back upon those days and scenes of youthful pride and ambition, with a feeling of awe and reminiscence, and wonder why and wherefore have I been spared through the labyrinth of time elapsed and for what, alas! I am wondering.

The most of the "Grays" left home for the scenes of the war in August, but I had not completed my arrangements and did not reach "Camp Burnett," Tennessee, until September 7. Now the most trying and impressing circumstances of these preparations was the last "goodbye" to my dear old mother and sweetheart, both of whom survived the war; the dear old mother greeting me on my return in a manner I shall leave to the imagination of you ladies to describe. I was her "baby" and had been mourned as lost more than once. But the sweetheart in the meantime had become the wife of another and gone to a distant State to make her home. Oh! the fickleness of woman and the uncertainties of war. Pardon me, ladies, I mean no reflection, but it hurts to this day; yet God in His wisdom and goodness knows I forgave her. Perhaps school day love is remembered and still lingers in the heart of some of those I am addressing, then she, at least, can appreciate this sentiment.

The 6th of September found me in this town (Paris, Ky.), where I began preparations for the life of a soldier, by substituting my "pumps" for "brogans," which I knew would be more suitable, really indispensable for a soldier on the march over rough and rugged roads. I sent back home my pumps and horse, the latter afterward confiscated and appropriated by the Yanks. Now I am sure my brogans presented a striking and ludicrous contrast to my "clawhammer" blue broadcloth and gold buttons, and to which I shall have occasion to refer again. But I was going to the war and why should I care for comment or criticism? That night found me in Louisville, a shy, cringing guest of the old Louisville Hotel, my brogans giving me more concern than anything else, being in such striking contrast to my clawhammer broadcloth and gold buttons. I recall the scenes of that night and next morning with a distinctness that makes me almost shudder to this day. If it were possible for you ladies to imagine the excitement of those days, filled with the thousands of exciting rumors that were heard every hour in the day, turn in whatever direction you might, and the clangor and preparation for war, you might have some idea of, and appreciate, my predicament. A solitary country boy, who had seen but little of the world, on his road south in quest of Southern rights on the field of battle. Were it not fraught with fearful recollections it would now seem ridiculous. But the night was spent, not in sleep, but in wild imaginings as to the outcome on the morrow and what the morning would develop.

Morning came and with reddened eyes and unsteady step, I came down the winding stairs of the old hotel, my mind filled with fearful misgivings. Going up to the office shyly I began instinctively to turn the leaves of the register; imagine my surprise when I read the names of Generals W. T. Sherman, L. J. Rousseau, Major Anderson of Fort Sumter fame and other Federal officers, aides and orderlies, who were stopping there; that humbug Kentucky "neutrality" no longer being observed. I was now almost ready to call on the Lord to save me. But my fears were intensified when a gentleman of middle age, whom I had noticed eyeing me closely, walked across the room, putting his hand on my shoulder and asked me to a corner of the room. "Angels and ministers of grace defend me" – in the hands of a detective. I'm gone now!

Noticing my look of fear and trepidation, he said, "Compose yourself young man, I am your friend – the shoes you wear (Oh, the tell-tale shoes! Why didn't I keep my pumps) lead me to believe you meditate joining the army, and if I am not mistaken you are aiming to go south to join the Confederates."

I was now halting between two opinions; was he aiming to have me commit myself, or was he really a friend? But proceeding, he said, "It is but natural you should suspect me, but I am your friend neverthe-less, and am here to advise and assist young men like you in getting through the lines (a somewhat calmer feeling came over me now) and you will have to be very cautious, for I fear your brogans are a tell-tale" – (I had already realized THAT). "You see," said, he, "excitement is running high and almost everybody is under suspicion, myself with others." I ventured to ask his name, which he readily gave me as Captain Coffee of Tennessee, to me a very singular name.

Feeling sure of his man and continuing, he said, "The train that leaves here this morning will likely be the last for the State line (and sure enough it was) and you will find excitement running high at the station; they have guards to examine all passen-gers and their baggage, and when you reach the station go straight to the ticket office, secure your ticket and go to the rear of the train. Go in and take the first vacant seat and for Heaven's sake, if possible, hide your brogans, for I fear they may tell on you." I had by this time become thoroughly convinced that he was really my friend and decided to take his advice.

But now the climax to the situation was, as I thought, about to be reached. Looking toward the winding stairs I saw coming down them (Coffee told me who they were) dressed in their gaudy regimentals (the regulation blue and gold lace), Generals W. T. Sherman and L. J. Rousseau, side by side, arm in arm, behind them the short, chubby figure of Major Anderson of Fort Sumter fame and some other prominent officers whose names I have forgotten, accompanied by their staff officers and orderlies. A "pretty kettle of fish" for me to be caught with – I thought. They passed into the dining room immediately. I shall never forget the hook-nose, lank, lean and hungry look of General Sherman, reminding me of Julius Caesar's description of Cassius. Later on I was often reminded of this incident, when Sherman was pushing us through Georgia, toward the sea in the celebrated campaign of '64. I was then almost wicked enough to wish that I had at this time and there ended his career. But, exchanging a few more words with Capt. Coffee, I called for my satchel and took the "bus" for the station; arriving there I acted upon the advice of my new made friend and adviser. Quickly procuring my ticket and entering the car, I secured the rear seat and with fear and trembling attempted to hide my brogans by setting my satchel on them. (We had no suit cases then.)

This was a morning of wonderful excitement in the station for it was the last train to leave Louisville for the State line and Memphis. There were thousands of people there crowding every available foot of space – excitement ran high. The train guards or inspectors – fully armed – were busy examining passengers and their baggage. My heart almost leaped from my bosom as they came down the aisle. But just before they reached the rear of the car the bell rang and the train started. The guards rushed for the door, leaving me and one or two others unquestioned and unmolested. Like "Paul, when he reached the three taverns," I thanked God and took courage. I doubt if the old station ever before or since saw such excitement and heard such a shout as went up from the people therein assembled as the train pulled out for Dixie. Many of these people were Southern sympathizers and wished us God-speed and a safe journey.

That evening I joined my schoolboy friends and soldier comrades, the "Flat Rock Grays," in Camp Burnett, Tennessee, the Grays dropping their name and acquiring the letter "H" in the regimental formation of that celebrated regiment commanded by Col. Robert P. Trabue and known as the Fourth Kentucky, C.S.A. That night I slept in camp for the first time – as to what I dreamed I am unable to say – it might have been of the sweetheart. The next day was spent in getting acquainted with the dear fellows whose comradeship I was to have and share for the next four years. Here began the experiences of the real soldier, that was to include some of the most momentous events in American history. Only one day, however, was spent in Burnett, for that night orders came for those companies that had been supplied with arms to break camp early next morning and take the train for Bowling Green – to "invade Kentucky." The companies without arms, among which was Company H, was to repair to Nashville where we procured arms, joining the rest of the regiment a few weeks later at Bowling Green.

I have told you of the beginning, now it is proper and altogether pertinent that I should refer to some of the closing scenes of my career as a soldier. But I am here leaving a gap in my history, the most important part of it, which will be found in other parts of this little book.

Having received my furlough at Jonesboro, where I was wounded on August 31, 1864, the following six months were spent in hospitals; first at Barnesville, later at Macon and then Cuthbert, Ga., and later still at Eufaula, Ala. I had as companions in hospital experiences three other Kentuckians, Captain E. F. Spears of this city, Paris, whom you all know to have been a gentleman of the highest honor and noblest emotions – a gentleman – Oh, how I loved him; and Lieutenants Hanks and Eales, noble fellows and companionable comrades. Here were formed ties of friendship – that death alone could sever.

But having sufficiently recovered from my wound, I decided the last of March that I would make an effort to reach my command (the Orphan Brigade) now engaged in a desperate effort to stay the progress of Sherman's devastating columns now operating in South Carolina.

The "Orphans" in the meantime and during my absence had been converted into cavalry. I was still on crutches and bidding Eufaula friends good-bye (with regret) I started once more for the front.

The times were now fraught with gloomy forebodings and misgivings, excitement running high. The South was in tears, terror stricken – the Confederacy surely and rapidly was reeling to her doom. General Wilson's cavalry was raiding through Alabama and Georgia with but little opposition, destroying the railroads and almost everything else of value as they moved across the country.

On the train I had very distinguished company in the person of General "Bob" Toombs, who commanded the Georgia militia, a mythical organization of the times, and Mrs. L.Q.C. Lamar of Mississippi, whose husband was afterward a member of Cleveland's Cabinet. I was very much impressed with the remarkable personality of this lady and felt sorry for her and her family of seven children, fleeing terror stricken from the raiders. Pandemonium seemed to reign supreme among these fleeing refugees, the air being literally alive with all sorts of rumors about the depredations and atrocities of the raiders. Numerous delays occurred to the train, everybody on board fearing the raiders and anxious to move on. General Toombs, excited and worried at these delays, determined to take charge of the situation and see that the train moved on. With a navy revolver in each hand he leaped from the train and with an oath that meant business said he would see that the train moved on – which it did rather promptly, the General taking due credit to himself for its moving, which the passengers willingly accorded him. Inquiring who this moving spirit was, I was told that it was General "Bob" Toombs (by this name, "Bob" Toombs, he was known throughout the United States). Instantly there flashed into my mind the celebrated speech he made in the United States Senate, in which he said that "ere long he expected to call the roll of his slaves beneath the shadow of Bunker Hill Monument" – and which speech did more to fire the hearts of the North than almost anything said or done prior to the war.

But finally we reached Macon – where I had been in the hospital – and on the afternoon of the second day after our arrival, Wilson's cavalry took possession of the city. That night some of the fiends, that are to be found in every army, applied the torch to the home of Senator Howell Cobb, the Lanier Hotel and a number of other prominent buildings. I could realize the excitement from the Confederate hospital on College Hill, which overlooks the city, and which was terrifying and appalling beyond anything I had ever before seen. The shrieks and cries of the women and children almost unnerved me. Woe of woes! Horror of horrors! I thought.

But I must do General Wilson the honor to say that he did not order or approve of this fiendish piece of work, for he did all in his power to prevent and stop it; and but for his efforts the city would no doubt have been completely destroyed.

Of course I abandoned my attempt to join the old boys of the "Orphan Brigade." I was now a prisoner, everything lost (save honor), gloom and chaos were everywhere. Obtaining a parole from the Federal officer in command (something new), I decided to join my comrades Knox and Harp, each of whom, like myself, had been put out of business by wounds received sometime before and who were sojourning with a friend in the country near Forsythe, intending to counsel with them as to the best course to be pursued next. Having enjoyed the hospitality of our host and his good wife for several days, Knox and myself decided to go down to Augusta for a last and final parting with the remnant of these dear "old boys" of the "Orphan Brigade" whom we learned were to be paroled in that city. We soon learned upon our arrival in the city that General Lewis and staff would arrive next morning. Next morning the General and staff rode through the city, the most sorrowful and forlorn looking men my eyes ever looked upon; it was enough to make a savage weep. The cause for which we had so long fought, sacrificed and suffered, lost, everything lost, God and the world apparently against us, without country, without home or hope, the old family being broken up and separated forever, our very souls sinking within us, gloom and sorrow overhanging the world; what would we do; what could we do? Learning from General Lewis that the remnant of the little band of immortals who had contributed so much to the history and renown of Kentucky in the great conflict would be paroled at Washington, some twenty miles from Augusta, Knox and myself proceeded to that place for a last and final farewell.

The associations of almost four years of the bloodiest war in modern times up to that day were here, to be forever broken up. The eyes that gleamed defiance in the battles' rage were now filled with tears of sorrow at parting. The hand that knew no trembling in the bloody onslaught now wavered and trembled – the hour for the last parting had arrived, the long struggle ended forever – good-bye, John; farewell, Henry; it is all over and all is lost, ended at last; good-bye, boys; good-bye.

Are their deeds worth recording, worth remembering? It is for you, dear ladies, rather than men, to say whether it shall be done or not, and in what way. I am content to leave it to you, knowing that it will be well and faithfully done.

Resuming the closing scenes of my experiences at Washington and the final sad leave-taking of these dear old "Orphans," I must revert to my friend and well wisher (as he proved to be), General Toombs.

The Confederate Government had saved from the ruin that befell and overtook it several thousand dollars in coin and which was being transported across the country, whither, no one seemed to know – in charge of a certain major.

Now Washington was the home of my hero of the train incident. The powers that were left decided to distribute a part of this coin among the faithful veterans who were being paroled at this point. The cavalry, who did not enlist until later in '62, receiving $26, in some instances more, while the Orphans received as their share only $3.50, a very unfair and inequitable distribution, character of service and time being considered. The cavalry in this, as in some other instances, receiving the lion's share and getting the most of the good things that fell to the lot of the "pooh" soldier. This money consisted mainly of "double eagles," three of which fell to the remnant of my company. The perplexing question now was how could we divide this money.

The matter was finally settled by the boys commissioning me to go down into the town (a mile or more away) to see if I could exchange it for smaller coins. Still on crutches, I finally consented, but it was a task. Going into town and from home to home – all business houses long since closed – I at last staggered on the home of General Toombs – not knowing he lived there. I recognized at once the moving spirit of the train incident. He and another gentleman were seated on the veranda engaged in earnest and animated conversation. Saluting in military style, I at once made known my business. The General protested that he had no change, but referring me to his guest, Major —, who, he said, was in charge of some funds in the house belonging to the government. The Major remarked if I would wait awhile he would furnish me with the required change, at the same time retiring to a back room of the house where I soon heard the sound of a hammer or hatchet, presumably in the hand of the Major, who was engaged in opening a box or chest. In the meantime the General invited me to a seat on the veranda and began plying me with numerous and pertinent questions – not giving me a chance to refer to the train incident – asking to what command I belonged, when and where I was wounded and how I expected to get home and many other questions, not forgetting in his vigorous and vehement way (for which he was noted) to deplore the fate of the Confederacy and denouncing the Yankee in unmeasured and vigorous terms.

Finally after so long a time the Major returned with the required change – all in silver and while not much, it gave me (already tired out) great worry before I reached camp on my crutches. Of course I thanked the Major and apologized for having put him to so much trouble, and saluting him good day, I started for the gate, the General preceding me and still asking questions. Opening the gate, for which I thanked him, I tipped a military salute and started up the sidewalk. But the General seemed very much interested in me and walking alongside the yard fence he suddenly thrust his hand into his vest pocket, pulling out a twenty dollar coin and quickly reaching across the fence, he said, "Here, Lieutenant, take this from me. You will doubtless need it." Dumfounded at this sudden change of affairs, I politely declined it, but the General, in a spirit of earnest command, forcefully said, "Here, take it, sir; you are a d—n long way from home and you will need it before you get there." Comprehending the spirit which prompted it, I accepted it and thanked him, extending him my hand, which he grasped with a warmth that thrilled my soul to its very depths.

Thus the diamond in the rough that I had seen on the train at once became the glittering jewel that sparkled and shed its brilliance to the depths of my then thankful and weary soul. I love to think of this incident and this great man (for he was truly a great man of his time), and transpiring at the time it did and under, to me, such distressing and discouraging circumstances, it is one of the happy and cheering oases of my soldier life.

Going from Washington back to Augusta I met and spent the following night in company with Hon. E. M. Bruce, one of the best friends I ever had, whose friendship, magnanimity and generosity toward myself and other Kentuckians was, as in my case, made practical, he presenting me with three double eagles, which I was compelled to receive as a recompense for acts of friendship and assistance rendered him during the trying times of the preceding four years. I have never known a grander character than E. M. Bruce, a truer friend, a nobler man.

But now, with more than $80 of real money, I was quite well equipped for the return to dear "Old

Kentucky," which I was glad to see after an absence of almost four years, spent under the most dangerous and trying circumstances to which it was possible for man to be exposed.

There were doubts in my mind as to what our status as citizens would be and just how we would be received and regarded by some – returning as we did, overcome, discomfited, defeated. But we well knew how we would be received by those who loved us and whose sympathies were manifested in a thousand ways not to be mistaken or misunderstood. Here in these manifestations was recompense for the long years of absence amid dangers, trials and suffering.

And now after a lapse of more than half a century, with its wonderful history, we are still remembered by some of the kind and gentle spirits that greeted us on our return, and other charming and lovely spirits of the U.D.C., descendants of the noblest ancestry that ever lived and inhabited this, the fairest land that God ever made.

These circumstances, these surroundings and inspiring scenes make hallowed the lives of these few surviving old veterans, rendering it a panacea for all that we as soldiers of the "lost cause" encountered and suffered.

From the fulness of my heart I thank you, noble ladies, for your kindness and patient attention. This opportunity to appear before you today is more than a pleasure and I feel honored to find myself in your presence and appreciate your happy greeting.

CHAPTER THREE

☆　☆　☆　☆

Recollections of the Battle of Shiloh

From an address delivered at the meeting of the
Morgan's Men Association at Olympian Springs,
September 2, 1916.

Mr. President, Old Comrades, Ladies and
Gentlemen:

I must confess that this is somewhat embar-
rassing attempting to talk in public at the age of
seventy-two, never having attempted such a thing
before. But the subject upon which I am expected to
talk is certainly, to myself, at least, interesting, and
the occasion I am sure is happy and inspiring, had I
only the ability to do them justice. However, by
reason of my inexperience in matters of this kind, I
believe I can safely appeal to the charity of my audi-
ence to overlook any failure I may make to properly
interest them in what I shall have to say.

You ask sir, that I shall relate some of my
observations and experiences of the great battle of

Shiloh. Well fifty-two years and more is a long time and takes us back to that important event in American History that transpired on the banks of the Tennessee on April 6 and 7, 1862. Some of these old veterans now seated before me can doubtless remember many of the exciting and intensely interesting scenes of these two eventful days. It is more deeply impressed upon my mind, because of the fact that it was our initial battle and early impressions are said to be always most lasting.

This was the first of a series of grand and important events in the history of that renowned little band of Kentuckians, known in history as the "Orphan Brigade," but which for the present occasion I shall designate as the Kentucky Brigade, it not receiving its baptismal or historic name until the celebrated charge of Breckinridge at Murfreesboro.

But what a grand and thrilling opening chapter in the lives of these Kentucky boys, as soldiers, for we were only boys, as we now look back at things, a majority of us being under twenty-one.

Now, if I were called upon to say which in my judgment was the best planned, most thoroughly and systematically, fought battle of the war in which I took part, I would unhesitatingly say Shiloh. As time rolled on and with subsequent observations and experiences on other important fields, such as Murfreesboro, Chickamauga, Resaca, Atlanta, Jonesboro and a number of others, I am still constrained to say that Shiloh was the typical battle. I mean, of course, battles fought in the West and in which Kentucky troops took a prominent part.

If in relating my story I shall seem somewhat partial to Kentuckians, I hope I may be excused for it is of them I shall talk mainly, besides, you know I love them dearly. And in the exercise of this partiality I claim to be justified from the fact that a number of the leading characters in this grand tragedy of war were Kentuckians. First among whom was the great general and peerless leader; others were Breckinridge, Preston, Tilghman, Trabue, Helm, Morgan, Monroe, Lewis, Hunt, Hodges, Wickliffe, Anderson, Burns, Cobb and last but by no means least, Governor George W. Johnson whose patriotic example was unsurpassed and whose tragic death was one of the most pathetic incidents of the great battle. A conspicuous figure indeed was he, so much so that when found on the field mortally wounded by the enemy, they believed him to be General Breckinridge. Private John Vaughn, of my old Company H of the Fourth Regiment, relates this story in regard to this sad and lamentable incident. Vaughn was severely wounded and was lying on the field near where Governor Johnston fell and from which he had just been removed by the enemy, when General Grant rode up and inquired to what command he belonged. When told by Vaughn to what command he belonged, Grant said: "And it is Kentuckians, is it, that have been fighting my men so desperately at this point?" Here is where the four desperate charges and counter-charges were made on the Seventh and noted by Colonel Trabue as commander of the Kentucky Brigade in his official report of the great battle, the bloodiest part of the field where Kentucky gave up many of her noblest and best. This is the field to which General Grant refers in his *Memoirs*, when in writing of the desperate fighting of the Confederates, he says: "I saw an open field on the second day's battle over which the Confederates had made repeated charges, so thickly covered with their dead that it might have been possible to have walked across the clearing in any direction stepping on dead bodies without touching a foot to the ground."

Here were enacted scenes of sublime courage and heroism that elicited the admiration and comment of the civilized world; here the soil of Tennessee drank freely the blood of her elder sister, Kentucky.

But Grant, when told by Vaughn that he belonged to the Kentucky Brigade, turned to one of his aids and ordered a litter to be brought and had Vaughn placed upon it saying, "We have killed your General Breckinridge and have him down yonder," pointing in the direction of their field hospital. He then had him taken down to where the supposed General Breckinridge lay. It seems that they were doubtful of and wished to establish his identity. Pointing to the body of the dying Governor he asked Vaughn if he was not his general. When Vaughn told him that it was Governor Johnson and not General Breckinridge, Grant turned away quickly with a look of disappointment upon discovering his mistake and learning who he was. Vaughn used to relate this incident with considerable feeling and pride as connecting him with General Grant at this particular time and under such peculiar and painful circumstances. I mention it because it contains more than ordinary interest to some of us Kentuckians, who had the opportunity of witnessing the heroic conduct and sublime courage of this noble citizen of Kentucky.

But let us notice while passing some of the sacrifices Kentucky made in this first great battle of the war in the West and the compliment incidentally and unintentionally paid us (as Kentuckians), by the greatest general that ever commanded the Federal army.

First among whom was the great general and peerless leader, Albert Sidney Johnston, whose name I always mention with feelings of profound pride and admiration (I would liked to have said veneration). George W. Johnson, the noble beloved citizen and patriotic Governor, whose voluntary example of sublime courage and heroism was without a parallel in the great battle. Thomas B. Monroe, the youthful and distinguished journalist, statesman and accomplished soldier, a man with scarce a peer at his age in either civil or military life. Charles N. Wickliffe, the gallant and dashing colonel of the Seventh Kentucky, and a thousand other Kentuckians many less distinguished but equally brave – the flower of Kentucky youth and manhood. Is it any wonder I am partial to Kentuckians and proud of their record in this great and memorable battle?

Oh, how well I remember the morning of that

eventful Easter Sabbath, April 6, 1862. So beautiful and lovely that all nature seemed proud and happy. Trees budding, flowers blooming, birds singing, everything seemingly joyful and happy in the bright sunshine of early spring, save man alone. But with what awfulness the scene changes when we contemplate man's actions at this hour and time bent upon the overthrow and destruction of his fellowman and how ominously significant the preparation.

Just at early dawn we were quietly awakened by our officers – many a noble and brave boy from his last sleep on earth; the bugle not sounding the reveille, for fear of attracting the attention of the enemy – it being part of the great general's plan to take him by surprise, which succeeded admirably, notwithstanding the oft repeated denials of General Grant to the contrary. Quickly arranging our toilets and having hastily despatched breakfast from our haversacks we formed in double column by company, the band in front leading, playing "Dixie," which sounded upon the early morning stillness in this deep wildwood, as it never before sounded, soul-stirring and inspiring. What patriotic soldier could fail to be moved by its charm and pathos? The veil of caution and silence now removed by the band, down through the woods of massive oaks we moved at quick-step, every man doubtless believing himself the equal of half a dozen Yankees. A very erroneous notion indeed, soon dispelled by hard and stubborn facts to the contrary. But on we moved, stopping but once to unsling knapsacks, which, with our Sunday clothes and precious jewels, we never saw again. Ah, some of those precious jewels! Still on we moved. Now the roll of the Skirmishers' rifles away out in front told that the issue of battle was being joined, not Greek against Greek, but American against American, in one of the most desperate and sanguinary conflicts of the great war. Led by two of the greatest military chieftains of the age, here the high spirited and chivalrous youth from the Southern plantations and the daring, hardy Western boy from the prairies of the West, had met in battle array.

Here was to be a display of courage and chivalry unsurpassed in the annals of war. Now an occasional boom, boom, of the big guns, began to echo up and down the valley of the Tennessee as Hardee's batteries seemingly in chorus with those of the enemy in reply, began to open on Grant's battalions now hurriedly forming, having recovered from their surprise caused by the sudden and unexpected attack of Hardee's advanced lines. Stirred by the highest ambition of our youthful hearts on toward the front rapidly and steadily, now in column of fours, moved the Kentucky Brigade. Passing down a little narrow valley just to the left and on the higher ground, we passed that gallant little band of Kentuckians known as Morgan's Squadron at the head of which, seated on "Black Bess" – the real (not the mythical "Black Bess" that some of you fellows sometimes talk so loudly about and never saw), but the real Black Bess – was that grandest specimen of a Kentucky soldier, save one – the immortal Breckinridge – Captain John H. Morgan. The Kentucky Brigade was proud to find itself in such noble, such royal company, though for a passing moment only. Oh, how it thrilled our hearts as these Kentucky boys, Morgan's men, greeted us by waving their hats, cheering and singing their famous battle song:

> Cheer, boys, cheer; we'll march away to battle;
> Cheer, boys, cheer, for our sweethearts
> and our wives;
> Cheer, boys, cheer; we'll nobly do our duty,
> And give to Kentucky our arms, our hearts,
> our lives.

General Duke, you remember this incident. Do you not, sir? More than happy am I with such a noble witness to attest the correctness of this part of my story. It was the second line of this famous stanza that touched my soul most and sunk deepest into my youthful heart, for I had left back in old Nicholas a little, black-eyed, curly-haired maiden whose image at that very moment seemed fairer than all the angels in heaven. My old heart still beats quick when I think of this thrilling incident and those charming eyes. Now there are doubtless some of you old veterans who are listening to me that left home under similar circumstances as myself, kissing farewell, as you thought, perhaps for the last time, the dear little girl you were leaving behind and who felt on the battle's verge as I did and was tempted to exclaim with me in the anguish of your heart, "Oh cruel, cruel relentless war, what sad havoc you have wrought with lovers and lovers' lives." Verily, old comrades, I believe I am growing sentimental as well as very childish, but these thoughts crowd my memory and must have vent. Still to the battle's breach I must go where the "pride, pomp and circumstances of glorious war" invite.

Pressing rapidly forward we quickly passed through the enemy's outer encampments from which they had fled when attacked and surprised by Hardee's Skirmishers, leaving behind them untouched, their breakfasts of steaming hot coffee, fried ham and other good things with which their improvised tables seemed to be heavily ladened, and which under other and more favorable circumstances, we would have quickly appropriated. But the scenes of greatest moment and absorbing interest were on the front toward which we were rapidly hurrying where the clash of steel, shot and shell was resounding with the fury of desperation.

How well I remember the first victim of war – a Confederate – I saw on this eventful morning. How well, too, I remember the hiss and scream of the first shells of the enemy's guns that passed closely above our heads, and how quickly and ungracefully we bowed in acknowledgment. How well, also, I remember the first volley fired at us by Colonel Worthington's Forty-sixth, Ohio, our neighbors from just across the river. We had hardly completed the formation of changing "front to rear" on our first company in order to confront them squarely by bringing our line parallel with theirs, when they opened fire on us, getting the drop on us, if you please.

Now I need not say much about this experience, for I am sure that every old veteran remembers well the first fire to which he was exposed, but I do believe that my hair must have stood on end and fairly lifted my cap for I felt as they leveled their rifles, that every man of us would surely be killed. Not many however, were killed or seriously hurt, for the enemy in their eagerness and great excitement fired wildly over our heads. The next was ours, and as we had been previously cautioned by Major Monroe to fire low, we made it count. Quickly reloading our rifles we had hardly fired the second volley when the sharp shrill voice of Major Monroe rang out amid the roar and din of battle, "Fix bayonet" and was quickly repeated by the company commanders. My, my; oh Lord; but the cold chills darted up and down my spinal column as I contemplated the use of the bayonet. Now if there is any scene upon the battle-field more exciting and more terrifying than the glimmer and glitter of a fixed bayonet in the hands of a desperate and determined enemy, pointed directly at your throat or your stomach, I have never seen it. Terrified at the gleam and clatter of our bayonets Worthington's men broke and fled through the woods rallying on their reserves, stationed some distance in rear of their original position. It was well perhaps for them that they did, for thoroughly drilled as we were in the bayonet exercise, they would doubtless have found themselves at a great disadvantage in the use of this weapon, had they stood to make the test. But with fixed bayonets, accelerated by the Rebel yell, we followed at a double-quick, passing over their dead and wounded halting just beyond.

What a ghastly sight; what a terrible scene! Here was pictured for the first time in our experience the horrors of the battle-field in all of its hideousness. How well the new Enfield rifles, with which we had been armed just before leaving Burnsville for the battlefield two days before, following the reading of General Johnston's famous battle order, were used upon this occasion, the dead and severely wounded of more than three hundred of the enemy grimly told. Colonel Trabue in his official report says more than four hundred but I hardly think there were so many. There were enough at least to attest the efficiency of our new Enfields and the correctness of our aim. Many of these poor fellows begged us piteously not to kill them as though we were a band of savages without pity or compassion, knowing nothing of the usages and customs of civilized warfare. It was an insult to our sense of honor and chivalry. But we soon convinced them by every act of kindness possible under the circumstances that we were both civilized and chivalrous, notwithstanding the teachings of the Northern press to the contrary. How false, absurd and ridiculous these charges by some of these stayed-at-home sycophants of the Northern press accusing us with brutal and inhuman treatment of their wounded that fell into our hands.

But, just before the encounter of the Fourth Kentucky, which occupied the extreme left of the Confederate battle line, with the Forty-sixth Ohio, the roll of musketry and the roar of artillery came down the battle line from right to left (a distance of more than three miles), like the successive waves of the ocean as Grant hurled his battalions in echelon against the extended lines of Johnston, opening fire in rapid succession as they deployed and struck our lines, to which, the Confederates in like successive manner instantly replied. Oh, I tell you this was sublimely grand beyond the power of man to describe. As Grant's battalions were successfully met and hurled back, that terrible and ominous sound, the "Rebel yell" heard by us for the first time on the battle field, told that the day was surely and steadily becoming ours. The enemy made another desperate and determined stand and from their advantageous position occupied by their reserves on which their broken columns had rallied, they poured a deadly and destructive fire into our ranks killing and wounding many of our men. We had been pushed forward under the enemy's fire and halted to await the movement of our reinforcements moving in our rear and to our left, and while awaiting the execution of this movement we learned quickly for the first time the importance of lying flat on our faces as a means of protection from this deadly fire of the enemy. This was trying indeed under orders not to fire; compelled to remain passive and see your comrades being killed all around you, momentarily expecting the same fate yourself. At last co-operating with the flanking column on our left, with fixed bayonets we made a desperate direct attack and drove the enemy from this very formidable position which they had been holding for some time – not, however, until we had lost in killed and wounded more than two score of our brave and gallant boys. I am now speaking of the operations of my own regiment – matters were too absorbing to pay much attention to what others were doing.

Again pushing forward we quickly encountered the enemy's reinforcements, which they had thrown forward to resist our advance and were again exposed to another scathing and deadly fire. Again resorting to our former tactics of lying flat on our faces, we returned their fire, turning upon our backs to reload our rifles, then again upon our faces to deliver fire. Here the battle raged furiously, for some time and here again we lost a number more of our gallant boys. I shall never forget the anguish of the boy immediately to my left, as he expired from the effects of a ball that passed through his body.

In the meantime and while the battle was raging at this point, Burns' and Cobb's Kentucky batteries of fourteen pieces, which were stationed upon the extreme right of the Kentucky Brigade, were hurling shot and shell, grape and canister, with terrific and deadly force into the enemy's moving columns, as they shifted from right to left of the battle line. Grant seemed anxious to turn our left, but was anticipated and promptly met by counter-movements of the Confederates, he having a most worthy rival in the art and skill of maneuvering troops upon the battlefield. Finally the terrible and desperate assault of the Tennesseans away to our right, led by the gallant Breckinridge and the peerless Johnston against the enemy's center and his stronghold, known as the "Hornet's Nest," compelled Grant to yield every position he had taken and seek shelter and protection under the banks of the Tennessee. This was the sad and fatal moment, for here in this desperate charge the great general fell.

Co-operating with the troops on our left the Kentucky Brigade hinged upon Burns' battery, the whole left wing of the army swinging like a massive gate to the right, joined in this last desperate charge and had the proud satisfaction of participating in the capture and impounding of Prentiss' division of more than three thousand men, including the celebrated Watterhouse battery of Chicago with its magnificent equipment of new guns and fine horses. This magnificent battery had been equipped by this great millionaire for whom it was named, and we wondered how he felt when he learned the fate of his pets. I never in my entire experience as a soldier saw such a humiliated and crestfallen body of soldiers as these men were; prisoners driving their own magnificent battery from the field. It looked really cruel to thus humiliate them. But then you know it is said, that all's fair in love and war. To the first of which saying I am compelled to demur for I know that all is not fair in love, however, it may be in war.

But in striking contrast, what a jubilant and over-joyed set of fellows we Confederates were, what a time for rejoicing!

This was one of the proudest moments of my soldier life, exciting and thrilling almost beyond de-scription. Their artillery being driven from the field by their own gunners; their infantry formed in a hol-low square stacking arms and lowering their colors; their officers dismounting and turning over their horses and side arms; Confederate officers and or-derlies galloping to and fro in every direction; ex-citement unbounded and uncontrolled everywhere. Imagine these transcendent and rapidly transpiring scenes and think for a moment if you can, how these "boys," unused to such tragedies, must have felt amid such stupendous and overwhelming surround-ings. Why we made the very heaven and earth trem-ble with our triumphant shouts. And I doubt not, I know they did, for General Grant intimates they did, the enemy routed and hurrying to the banks of the Tennessee for protection, trembled also.

Now the scene changes somewhat, reforming our lines and filing to the right and left around this enclosed square in which these prisoners were held, we again moved forward to the front expecting to deliver the last and final blow. Four o'clock, three-quarters of an hour later, with more than two hours of sunshine in which to deliver the last and final blow, found us drawn up in the most magnificent line of battle I ever beheld, extending up and down the river bottom to the right and left as far as we could see, straight as an arrow; every man in place standing at "attention," exuberant with joy, flushed with victory, all understanding the situation, eager for the signal to be given that they knew would finish the glorious day's work. Grant's army cowering beneath the banks of the Tennessee awaiting the final summons to surrender. What a moment of grand anticipation and oh, how quick the heart beat! But at what fearful cost to the Confederate cause, the apparent great victory! The voice of the great commander, now silent with a successor unwilling to finish the day's work so gloriously begun and so successfully executed up to the hour of his fall. And oh, how important the hour to the new born nation! How portentous the signs! Here and in this hour was sacrificed the opportunity of the Southland's cause, here was thrown away, so to speak the grandest opportunity ever offered to any general in modern times. Here the "green-eyed monster," jealousy, must have whispered into the ear of Beauregard. Here I must draw the black curtain of disappointment and despair to which I never can be reconciled. But let it rest as lost opportunity and bury it in the oblivion of forgetfulness. Paradoxically speaking here was lost the opportunity of the "Lost Cause." But what followed, many, yes all of us know too well.

It is strange what momentous events sometimes turn upon seemingly trifling and insignificant circumstances. With the prevailing tenseness of the moment, if one man had leaped to the front of that battle line and shouted "forward," Grant's army as

a consequence would have been overrun and captured. Grant known no more in history; the "Stars
and Bars" would have been planted upon the banks
of the Ohio; Kentucky redeemed and history differently written. Had Johnston the great captain, lived,
this would have been accomplished. But it seems
that Providence decreed it otherwise by removing
the master mind.

From this magnificent battle line which I
have attempted to describe, and this moment of
proud hope and expectancy, we were, by order of
Beauregard, withdrawn to the camps of the enemy
from which we had driven them during the day – not
worn out and exhausted – which Beauregard gave as
his excuse for failing to carry out the plans of the
great commander to crush Grant before Buell could
come to his rescue.

Passing the night in the camps of the enemy;
recounting the exciting incidents of the day; indulg-
ing in the rich and bountiful supplies of a plethoric
commissary, and no less rich and bountiful supply of
sutlers stores in great variety, just received from the
North, we enjoyed a "Balshazzar" feast, not knowing, and little thinking of the "handwriting on the
wall" in the form of 30,000 reinforcements then
crossing the Tennessee to be met and reckoned with
on the morrow.

Why, oh why, did Beauregard not allow us to
finish the day's work so gloriously begun by Johnston? Every man must answer this question for himself. Beauregard did not answer it satisfactorily to the

soldiers who were engaged, whatever the opinion of the world. What, but the spirit of envy and jealousy and an overweening ambition to divide the honors of victory with Johnston, which he hoped and expected to win on the morrow, could have controlled his course? That and that alone, answers the sad question in the mind of your humble friend and comrade. I am aware that this will be considered presumption in me, but it is history in part and as observer and participant, I have the right to criticize.

The morning of the fateful 7th came and with it the direful results that followed. The arrival of Buell, the Blucher of the day, turned the tide and sealed the fate of the cause – the golden opportunity lost, lost forever! The history of that day is well known to all students of the great war and to none better than the few survivors of that little band of Kentuckians afterward known in history as the Orphan Brigade, and whose part in the grand tragedy was such an important factor. It needs no studied eulogium or lofty peroration to tell the story of the part played by this little band. A loss of forty per cent in killed and wounded tells the story, and is the panegyric offered by Kentucky on this memorable and bloody field.

I might speak more in detail of this last day's bloody work and describe more at length many of the horrible sights witnessed and the terrible suffering of our wounded in their transfer to Corinth during the next three days over almost impassable roads – the most horrible the mind could possibly picture, exposed to the almost continuous downpour of rain and the awful, awful sadness that filled our hearts in the loss of so many of our comrades, kinsmen and school-fellow friends, and the further deep humiliation of final defeat, but the story would be too horrible and sad to elaborate.

I have already taken too much of your time in relating a little of personal romance in connection with something of history and in conclusion will say I am here in part for what may be, though I hope not, a last farewell handclasp with these dear "Old Boys," Morgan's men, the equals of whom as soldiers and citizens, Kentucky and the world will never again see. I thank you for your attention and the courtesy you have shown me.

It seems altogether natural and opportune now that a large part of the world is engaged in war that our minds should revert to the past and the historic battle scenes in which we engaged should be renewed in reminiscence.

CHAPTER FOUR

☆　☆　☆　☆

The Bombardment of Vicksburg

Because of the similarity of scenes now transpiring on the Western front in France I am tempted
to describe a scene that occurred, and that I witnessed, during the siege of Vicksburg in July, 1862.
My regiment (4th Ky.) had been detailed and sent on
detached service down to Warrenton, some miles
below Vicksburg, leaving in camp a number of sick
that were unable to go, among whom was Capt.
Bramblett and myself. On the morning of the 15th of
July just at sunrise, suddenly, unexpectedly, as if the
infernal regions had suffered an eruption, the earth
rocked and trembled, the heavens seemed pierced
and rent with the roar and thunder of cannon of all
sizes, mortars from gunboats, siege guns, land batteries and everything of a terrifying and destructive
character that man was capable of inventing, appeared to be turned loose, an explanation of which
no one would venture to make.

Directly however, news came that the Confederate ram *Arkansas* had run the blockade of the upper fleet of Federal gunboats and transports, and was lying at the wharf in Vicksburg. The news was magical on some of us sick fellows, and myself and Sergeant Knox started immediately, without breakfast, to see the wonder and learn the news of the exciting episode. Arriving at the wharf we soon saw the cause of the terrible outburst of excitement and terror.

The *Arkansas* had been constructed at Yazoo City. Whisperings of its existence and probable descent upon the blockading fleet in the Mississippi had been heard for some time, and now we could see the monster (so to speak) in her grim and battered condition with numerous holes in her smoke stack, made by shots from the enemy's guns, and a large piece torn out of her cast prow. Her crew was composed of the most daring, despicable, smoke-begrimed looking set I ever beheld, but who were elated at their successful victory. It was both interesting and amusing to hear them discussing their recent experiences.

That night the world went wild and pandemonium reigned supreme in and around Vicksburg; for every gun and mortar in both the upper and lower fleets turned loose every element of hell and terror they possessed, with the seeming determination to destroy everything in and around the devoted old city. The Confederate siege-guns with "Whistling Dick" for leader joining in the grand orchestral chorus of ruin and chaos.

The scene was the most spectacular and pyrotechnical event of the war and has never been equaled unless it has occurred in the awful experiences on the Western front or at the Dardanelles. It was sublimely grand and tests the wildest imagination of the mind to describe it.

The air was literally burdened, with ascending and descending shells which were easily traced in their course upward and downward, shells from the upper and lower fleets, crossing each other in their flight heavenward, before they reached their zenith, others in their downward course and a few at the apex, and still others that failed to explode reached the ground destroying everything with which they came in contact. The flashes from these guns illumined the surroundings for miles, and reminded you of a terrific thunderstorm with continuous flashes of lightning. Every color of the rainbow could be seen in this terrible and grand display. Balloon shaped clouds of smoke from exploding shells could be seen, floating slowly, softly, through the air, adding amazement and wonder to the grand aerial tragedy taking place in the heavens.

In reading of the terrific bombardments in the great war now raging, and comprehending these descriptions and pictures, I count myself no stranger, and this scene I have attempted to describe I am sure will compare favorably with anything in the great world-war of today. Not all the wonders and terrors of war are yours, boys! Some of us older warriors

have seen something of war too. But it's all grand
and glorious, isn't it boys?

CHAPTER FIVE

☆ ☆ ☆ ☆

Murfreesboro (Stone River)

It is to the great and interesting battle of Murfreesboro and some of the incidents and circumstances preceding it, that I shall devote this article. History will some day accord it but one name, whereas it now has two – Murfreesboro and Stone River – but I shall use the former.

Here a mile or so southeast of the city, on a beautiful little plain or suburban scope of country, was encamped for a period of three months, the Orphan Brigade. The weather was beautiful and we enjoyed both it and the many good things we had to eat and the hospitable greetings of the good people of the town and surrounding country. But while we were enjoying these good things, we were undergoing a strict military training, being drilled in the school of the company, battalion and the more comprehensive and enlarged movements of the brigade and division maneuvers, some of which we had seen employed at Shiloh and elsewhere by exigencies in actual battle. It was a matter of general pride in which as a member, I still glory that the Orphan Brigade was the most thoroughly drilled and best disciplined body of men in the Confederate army. In substantiation of this claim, I refer to the compliment paid us a little later on by General Hardee, in a trial drill with the First Louisiana Brigade, held at Beech Grove in the spring following, and at which trial drill General Hardee was one of the judges, and was heard to say that to excel our drilling would require the construction of a different and better code than was laid down in the system of tactics bearing his name. The truth was we were determined to allow no body of troops to excel us in anything pertaining to these accomplishments or history of the soldier. This was accomplished in a great measure by the requirements and training of that military martinet, "Old" Roger Hanson. I use the appellation with the most profound respect. The facts as to these accomplishments can be attested by numbers of men still living and who often refer to General Hanson's rigid discipline and requirements with feelings of respect and pride. I must instance one circumstance, in support of this assertion.

Some time after he took command he issued an order that all officers and privates alike should be in full dress and in proper places at roll call in the morning after the sounding of the reveille. This did not suit many of the officers who wanted to take a morning snooze, but "Roger's" orders were inexorable to officers and soldiers alike and it was for a few mornings laughable to see these officers hustling on their clothes and into line. There was nothing that pertained to discipline and order that escaped his notice. It was sometimes amusing to hear some fellow relate his experience in attempting to outwit and fool him, and the fellow that attempted it was always caught. It just could not be done.

But the whirligig of time was rapidly turning and bringing with it lively and exciting times – big with importance to the country and the Confederate cause and especially and particularly to these dear Orphans of mine.

While in Mississippi and preceding his disastrous Kentucky campaign and in which his malevolent nature was displayed, Bragg refused us the great joy we so earnestly and hopefully prayed for, viz, the return to Kentucky with his army, where we might see the dear ones at home, and incidentally aid the cause by inducing enlistments.

But the fact that quite a number of our fellow Kentuckians were coming out with the newly enlisted cavalry commands and bringing with them the news from home and friends – the first of consequence for a year or more – gave us some comfort and consolation. In the meantime some interesting matters of thrilling moment were transpiring down here, "Where the oak, the ash and red elm tree, all grow green in old Tennessee."

Rosecrans, not satisfied with results at Perryville, was cutting across the country for another opportunity to test his military skill and prowess, and to punish these unrepentant rebels for daring to offer resistance to the "old flag" and trying to "break up the best Government the world ever saw," and over which Government some of these same people are now fussing among themselves.

Excuse me, please. I see I am again off my base. Back to my beloved Orphans I must go. Oh, how I do love them!

The change from the ordinary routine of drill maneuver and review was brought about by the plan of General Morgan to attack the enemy's advance post at Hartsville, north of the Cumberland and about thirty miles or more from Murfreesboro. This movement included in its plan the co-operation of the Orphan Brigade and making it a distinctly Kentucky command, planned, led and fought by Kentuckians, and which was one of the most complete and brilliant affairs of the war. Some of us to this day feel the sting of disappointment of not being privileged to share in this *"coupe de grace,"* as the Fourth and Sixth Regiments were left at Baird's mill to guard against the possibility of an intercepting column from Nashville. My heart went out in sympathy (practically) to these boys on their return to our encampment, worn out with fatigue, exhausted and hungry and almost frozen, the weather being bitter cold and the ground covered with snow to a depth of several inches. I confess also to a feeling of sorrow for the poor blanketless prisoners who passed a night of suffering, though we did the best we could for them by furnishing them with fires.

But here again the Orphans engaged in this fight paid dearly for their honors, especially the Second Regiment, which lost heavily in both officers and men, the Ninth Regiment also losing considerable. But this seemed but the prelude to the grand Christmas entertainment staged to come off later and when Breckinridge's Kentuckians received the soubriquet Orphan Brigade by which they have ever since been known and which will pass into the annals of history, alongside that of the "Tenth Legion," the "Old Guard" and "Light Brigade."

With a sense of feeling that impresses me with my utter inability to at all do justice to the subject of Murfreesboro (or Stone River), I fear to undertake the task.

To the writer this was in some respects one of the most interesting, exciting and captivating battles of the war in which he took part. Captivating, because the great battle of the 31st was witnessed from my vantage point of view – the left of our entrenchments on Swain's Hill – overlooking the stretch of country on which the battle was fought, extending as it did from the Nashville turnpike and railroad, which at this point are parallel, and at which point also stood the famous "Cowans' burnt house," referred to by historians and which I saw burn the afternoon before. From this knoll I could see the principal part of the field.

Before attempting to describe the battle on this part of the field, I must look up my Orphans and see what they are now, and have been doing these last few hours. On the afternoon of Monday, the 29th they took possession of this hill, which was the acknowledged key to Bragg's position of defense. And herein lies a kind of mystery, why he would trust to these men, in the judgment of whose officers he showed later on he had so little confidence, this the most important point in his whole line, and why should it be entrusted to them – the Kentucky Brigade. Some were wicked enough to say, and his course toward us later, as that of Friday, strengthens this belief that he wanted us all killed, hence placing us in the most perilous position. Now mind you, gentle reader, I am not giving this as my opinion, but others have given it as theirs. While "bivouacking" a little behind this hill the enemy's skirmishers a little after dark made quite a determined onset on our skirmishers in front of the hill, but were driven back finally with considerable loss to both parties. It was a daring and courageous move and created no little excitement and concern and looked for a time like a night attack was pending. The 30th was spent in getting ready by both parties to the battle.

And early on the morrow we took our position on Swain's Hill in support of Cobb's and the Washington artillery. From my vantage position I could see more plainly the Confederate lines than the Federal, because the Confederates were on a direct line extending southward, while the Federals were obliquely to the front and partially obscured by an intervening cedar glade and in the afternoon the

Confederates swung like a great gate on their pivotal position, while just behind and to the left of this was the enemy's strong point of resistance, to which he had finally been driven. The smoke from the guns of the long lines of infantry, as they moved forward to the attack and the counter stroke from the enemy's resisting columns, the dashing to and fro, up and down the lines and over the field by officers, orderlies, aides and couriers, carrying orders and dispatches, with here and there a battery belching forth shot and shell was a sight wonderful to behold and never to be forgotten. The most thrilling incident to that view was early in the day when a body of cavalry, supposed to be "Dragoons," swung into line from behind the cedar glade with drawn sabers, gleaming and waving in the crisp chill sunlit air, dashed down over the open fields in a grand charge upon the Confederate infantry, whose movements a few moments before convinced me of this approaching cavalry charge.

We had been instructed by Buckner, Monroe and others on the drill field in the formation of the "hollow square" to resist the charge of cavalry and when I saw these regiments doubling column at half distance I knew what was coming. To see the field officers on horseback rushing within the squares as they closed and the front rank kneeling, all with fixed bayonets glittering in the frosty sunlight, and these oncoming charges with waving sabers and glittering helmets was a sight unsurpassed by anything I witnessed during the war. The nearest approaching it was by Sherman's charge at Resaca. As soon as the squares were formed the artillery in the rear opened fire through these intervening spaces made by the formation of the square, whereupon artillery and infantry combined swept the field and the charging column turned in confusion and route, skurrying helter skelter back over the field, leaving numbers of men horseless.

Soon the "Rebel yell" down the line told us that things were going our way and looking we could see our friends moving forward like a mighty serpent drawing his coils.

While this was transpiring on the left a battery in our front on the opposite side of the river was industriously employed in shelling Cobb's and Slocum's batteries stationed on Swain's Hill, and whose business for the time it was the Orphans to support. When I saw this cavalry charge, to which I have referred, the thought instantly and involuntarily came to my mind of the repeated attacks of Napoleon's cavalry on the squares of Wellington's infantry at Waterloo. The sight was so thrilling that I hoped they would repeat it. But how foolish, I thought this was, in this body of cavalry attempting to ride down regiments of veteran infantry. Their officers must surely have thought that they could reach the Confederate line before they could complete this formation. If so, they paid dearly for their mistake.

The battle progressed steadily and satisfactorily to the Confederates until about four o'clock, when they, in the language of the "bum," "run against a snag." Woods' and Sheridan's divisions, with other of Rosecrans' forces, had concentrated upon his extreme left, which was his strongest position for a final and last stand. The conflict here was desperate and bloody, neither party seeming to have much the advantage.

The National cemetery now occupies this identical ground and in which there are more than 6,000 Federal soldiers buried. A beautiful and fit place for the remains of these brave Western soldiers to rest, for here upon this field was displayed a courage that all men must admire.

Both armies slept that night upon the field with the greater part of the field in possession of the Confederates and the advantages and results of the day almost wholly in their favor.

The Orphans spent the night in the rear of and among the artillery they had been supporting. When morning came we found that the enemy was still in our front instead of on the road to Nashville as Bragg believed. Both parties seemed willing that a truce should prevail for the day and scarcely a shot was heard. Bragg believed that Rosecrans' army was "demolished" and would surely retreat to his base (Nashville), and so informed President Davis.

But old "Rosy" had something else in his mind. He was planning and scheming and matured a plan for a trap and Bragg walked right into it with the innocence of a lamb and the ignorance of a man that had never known anything of the art of war, and the butchery of the next day followed as a result of his obstinacy and the lack of military skill. Had he listened to the protestations of General Breckinridge and his officers he might have saved for the time being his military reputation and the lives of several hundred brave and noble men.

The recounting of the steps that led up to this ill-conceived and fatal denouement and the efforts by General Breckinridge to prevent its consummation, by one while not high in rank, but who claims to know something of the facts in the case, may not go amiss even at this late day.

Early on the morning of January 2, Captain Bramblett, commanding Company H, Fourth Kentucky, and who had served with General Breckinridge in Mexico, received orders from him (Breckinridge), to make a thorough reconnaissance of the enemy's position, Company H being at that time on the skirmish line. Captain Bramblett with two of his lieutenants, myself one of them, crawled through the weeds a distance of several hundred yards to a prominent point of observation from which through his field glass and even the naked eye we could see the enemy's concentrated forces near and above the lower ford on the opposite side of the river, his artillery being thrown forward and nearest to the river. His artillery appeared to be close together and covering quite a space of ground; we could not tell how many guns, but there was quite a number. The infantry was seemingly in large force and extended farther down toward the ford. Captain Bramblett was a man of no mean order of military genius and information, and after looking at, and studying the situation in silence for some minutes, he said to us boys, "that he believed Rosecrans was setting a trap for Bragg." Continuing, he said, "If he means to attack us on this side, why does he not reinforce on this side? Why concentrate so much artillery on the bluff yonder? He must be expecting us to attack that force yonder, (pointing to Beatty's position on the hill north of us,) and if we do, he will use that artillery on us as we move to the attack."

At another time during the afternoon I heard him while discussing the situation with other officers of the regiment use substantially the same argument. I accompanied Captain Bramblett to General Breckinridge's headquarters and heard him make substantially in detail a report containing the facts above recited. Captain Tom Steele was ordered (his company having relieved ours) on the skirmish line to make a reconnaissance also, and made a similar report, and lastly General Breckinridge, to thoroughly and unmistakably understand the situation and satisfy himself, in company with one or two of his staff examined the situation as best he could and I presume reached the same conclusion, and when he (Breckinridge) repaired to Bragg's headquarters and vouchsafed this information and suggested the presumptive plan of the enemy, Bragg said: "Sir, my information is different. I have given the order to attack the enemy in your front and expect it to be obeyed."

What was General Breckinridge to do but attempt to carry out his orders, though in carrying out this unwise and ill-conceived order it should cost in one hour and ten minutes 1,700 of as brave and chivalrous soldiers as the world ever saw. What a terrible blunder, what a bloody and useless sacrifice! And all because General Breckinridge had resented the imputation that the cause of the failure of Bragg's Kentucky campaign was the "disloyalty of her people to the Confederate cause." Could anyone of the thousands of Kentuckians that espoused the cause of the South, complacently acquiesce in this erroneous charge and endorse the spirit that prompted this order and led to the slaughter of so many of her noble boys? This was the view that many of us took of Bragg's course.

How was this wicked and useless sacrifice brought about? "That subordinate must always obey his superior" – is the military law. In furtherance of Bragg's order we were assembled about three o'clock on the afternoon of January 2, 1863 (Friday, a day of ill luck) in a line north of and to the right of Swain's Hill, confronting Beatty's and Growes' brigades, with a battery or two of artillery as support. They being intended for the bait that had been thrown across the river at the lower ford, and now occupied an eminence some three-quarters of a mile to the right-front of the Orphan's position on Swain's Hill.

This was the force, small as it was that Bragg was so anxious to dislodge. Between the attacking line and Federal position was a considerable scope of open ground, fields and pastures, with here and there a clump of bushes or briars, but the entire space was in full view of and covered by the enemy's batteries to the left of the line on the opposite side of the river previously referred to. If the reader will only carry these positions in his eye, he can readily discover the jaws of the trap in this murderous scheme.

A more imposing and thoroughly disciplined line of soldiers never moved to the attack of an enemy than responded to the signal gun stationed immediately in our rear, which was fired exactly at four o'clock. Every man vieing with his fellowman, in steadiness of step and correct alignment, with the officers giving low and cautionary commands, many knowing that it was their last hour on earth, but without hesitating moved forward to their inevitable doom and defeat. We had gotten only fairly started, when the great jaws of the trap on the bluff from the opposite side of the river were sprung, and bursting shells that completely drowned the voice of man were plunging and tearing through our columns, ploughing up the earth at our feet in front and behind, everywhere. But with steadiness of step we moved on. Two companies of the Fourth regiment, my own and adjoining company, encountered a pond, and with a dexterous movement known to the skilled officer and soldier was cleared in a manner that was perfectly charming, obliquing to the right and left into line as soon as passed.

By reason of the shorter line held by the enemy, our line, which was much longer and the colors of each of our battalions being directed against this shorter line, caused our lines to interlap, making it

necessary, in order to prevent confusion and crowding, that some of the regiments halt, until the others
had passed forward out of the way. When thus halted they would lie down in order to shield themselves
from the enemy infantry fire in front, who had by
this time opened a lively fusillade from behind their
temporary works.

While lying on the ground momentarily a very
shocking and disastrous occurrence took place in
Company E, immediately on my left and within a few
feet of where I lay, a shell exploded right in the middle of the company, almost literally tearing it to
pieces. When I recovered from the shock, the sight
I witnessed was appalling. Some eighteen or twenty
men hurled in every direction, including my dear
friend, Lieut. George Burnley of Frankfort. But these
circumstances were occurring every minute now
while the battle was raging all around and about us.
Men moved intuitively – the voice being silenced by
the whizzing and bursting shells. On we moved,
Beatty's and Growes' lines giving way seemingly to
allow the jaws of the trap to press with more and ever
increasing vigor upon its unfortunate and discomfited
victims. But on we moved until the survivors of the
decoy had passed the river and over the lines stationed on the other side of the river, when their new
line of infantry opened on our confused and disordered columns another destructive and ruinous fire.

Coupled with this condition and correlative to
it, a battery of Growes and a part of their infantry
had been cut off from the ford and seeing our con-

fused condition, rallied, reformed and opened fire on our advanced right now along the river bank. Confronted in front by their infantry, with the river intervening; swept by their artillery from the left and now attacked by both infantry and artillery by an oblique fire from the right, we found ourselves in a helpless condition, from which it looked like an impossibility to escape; and but for the fact that two or three batteries had been ordered into position to check the threatened advance of the enemy and thereby distract their attention, we doubtless would have fared still worse.

We rallied some distance to the right of where we started and found that many, very many, of our noblest, truest and best had fallen. Some of them were left on the field, among whom was my military preceptor, advisor and dear friend, Captain Bramblett, who fell into the hands of the enemy and who died a few days after in Nashville. I shall never forget our parting, a moment or two before he received his wound – never forget the last quick glance and the circumstances that called it forth. He was a splendid soldier and his loss grieved me very much. Many another gallant Kentuckian, some of our finest line and field officers, were left on the field, a sacrifice to stupidity and revenge. Thirty-seven per cent in one hour and ten minutes – some say one hour – was the frightful summary. Among the first of these was the gallant and illustrious Hanson, whose coolness and bearing was unsurpassed and whose loss was irreparable. He with Breckinridge understood and was fully sensible of – as indicated by the very seriousness of his countenance – the unwisdom of this move and as shown in their protest to Bragg. What a pity that a strict observance of military rule compelled it to be obeyed against his mature military mind and judgment, causing the loss of such a magnificent soldier and gentleman – uselessly and foolishly.

Contemplating this awful sacrifice, as he rode by the dead and dying in the rear of our lines, General Breckinridge, with tears falling from his eyes, was heard to say in tones of anguish, "My poor Orphans! My poor Orphans!" little thinking that he was dedicating to them a name that will live throughout the annals of time and crown the history of that dear little band with everlasting immortality.

I have tried to give you above a description from memory's tablet of the battle of Murfreesboro, and I shall now relate some of my observations made on my recent visit together with further references, to the events that transpired on that eventful field – the study of which is of almost overwhelming interest.

A Visit to Murfreesboro in 1912

Here, as elsewhere and on other fields, the view is especially and particularly interesting, because of the country being more level and more open with the view much less obstructed. It was worth a half dozen years to live over, in reminiscence, this week of intense excitement, interest and danger. And here too, as at Chickamauga, memory refused to be satisfied, and I find myself wishing I could see it again. I feel that I could never tire looking at the different aspects of the view and studying the tragic scenes as they transpired on this eventful closing of this eventful year of 1862, and the no less eventful opening of the year 1863. To those who lived in this historic decade and participated in these events of bygone years are of intense and ever thrilling interest, but few realize that these things happened a half century ago.

Here as elsewhere events came back to me and I had but little or no difficulty in locating the leading and many of the minor places of interest.

The immediate vicinity of our long encampment is changed considerably by houses being erected nearby and on the ground where our camps stood, but the big spring house, however, still does duty as of yore. The place on the Shelbyville turnpike where we held guard mount and review is much changed. So also are the grounds on the east side of the city where we held brigade and division drill, it now being "built up." But one of the leading landmarks of the town and of special interest to the Orphans and other Kentuckians is still intact and but little changed in appearance, but now used for a different purpose. I refer to the Judge Ready residence where General Morgan captured his grand prize. There is not an old Orphan now living, that does not remember how he used to primp for the march by this house, and how proudly he stepped and with what perfect mien he marched to Billy McQuown's best pieces, all to have the privilege of "showing off," and having the opportunity for a sly glance at the beautiful Queen sisters standing on the upper veranda. You know, old boys, just how this was, don't you?

But my mind is taking me back to the battle-field where the things of real excitement were tran-spiring, where "the pride, pomp and circumstances of glorious war are to be found."

Starting out in company with Rev. Everett Smith, we took the Nashville pike crossing the river at the same place we crossed when on the retreat from Bowling Green to Shiloh in February, 1862, and where I had crossed several times while en-camped later near the town, and over and beyond which I saw the celebrated cavalry charge and the victorious columns of the Confederates move on December 31. My mind was so completely occupied and crowded that I scarcely knew what to do or say. I know I must have been a study, to my young friend for a time at least.

I could see again in imagination the smoke and red fire and could hear the crackling flames as they leaped high in air of the famous "Cowan" house as we rode by. I imagined as we rode on that I could hear the yells and shouts of the contending lines as they surged forward and across the turnpike to the famous cut in the railroad, where Wood and Sheridan saved the day to the Federals against the last grand charge of Cleburne, Preston and Pillow of the Confederates.

As before stated, here is a fitting place for the six thousand Federals who rest here. Here at the cemetery, I was introduced to Captain Thomas, the officer in charge, who was exceedingly polite and courteous and whom I found by conversing with, that I had faced at Shiloh and who had the most perfect recollection of many of the chief points and incidents of that battle. I regretted very much that I could not spend more time with him, as he impressed me as being a man after my own heart. But my young friend and myself had promised to be back at the dinner hour and I was therefore compelled to close my interview.

I spent the afternoon in glancing over town and meeting and conversing with old soldiers and others whom I found interested in my mission, and willing and anxious to give me any information I desired.

I met and arranged with Captain Mitchell, who now owns a part of the field over which the celebrated charge of Breckinridge was made, to go out with me next morning and in company with him and a young friend, W. H. Hohgatt, of Pittsburgh, Pa. We started early, going over the same road, crossing the same bridge, as the day before to a point near the cemetery where the road to McFadden's ford leaves the turnpike and runs north by the bluff – the famous bluff where Rosecrans' fifty-eight pieces of artillery were stationed that wrought such dreadful havoc upon Breckinridge's men as they moved across the fields to attack Beatty and Growes (the decoy) on the other side of the river. Here we crossed the river at the lower ford, so famous in history but which is properly known as McFadden's. Here we "tied up" and in company with my companions we took to the fields and woods, which latter exist now in fancy only. Up the gradual slope we went to the crest of the ridge (now a cotton patch) to where Beatty and Growe were stationed, swinging around as we went to the point overlooking the river on which stood the massive oaks where the Sixth Kentucky, led by that incarnate demon of war, "Old Joe" Lewis, with flashing sword and blazing eyes, more terrible than the eyes of a raging lion and who impressed me as I was never impressed before or since, with the devil in human form. He presented a picture at that time I shall never forget. It is as grimly and immovably fixed in my mind as the sun and the stars and I become enthusiastic whenever I think of him and the incident. Then we moved along the crest northward to the point where the Fourth Kentucky struck Beatty's line. Looking east and south towards the Lebanon pike, we could see the vicinity where we started in the charge about midway between the crest and the pike. Turning around we could look down the north slope of the ridge and over which we pressed Beatty and the right of Growes' brigade to McFadden's ford, dropping into, as we moved down the narrow sag or depression that leads from the top of the hill straight to the ford and which furnished the only protection from the murderous fire of the fifty-eight guns massed on the bluff. Out of this depression, going or coming, we were exposed to this dreadful and incessant fire. Opposite to and some forty yards from this ford is the picket fence where we were compelled to halt and which is so well remembered by many of the Orphans.

The Federals passed around the end of this fence, they being acquainted with the situation, but we struck it square and were compelled to halt. Just outside and along this picketing were piled the enemy's drums and upon which the minnie balls from their new and supporting line on the opposite side of the river were beating a funeral dirge for many of our dear boys who were here compelled to halt and die to no purpose whatever. I walked along this picket fence, which looks just as it did then, but of course has been rebuilt, and over the very ground on which my dear Captain Bramblett fell and with whom I exchanged glances a moment before. To give expression to my feelings as I contemplated this last glance, this look in life at my dear friend and leader was impossible and I turned away with sickened heart from the fatal spot and retraced my steps over the field to the rallying point, every step of the way marked by exploding shells and flying shot from the enemy's battery of fifty-eight guns which seemed determined to show no mercy at all.

Lest some one may say I am magnifying this story of the "battery on the bluff" I will quote here verbatim from the tablet on the twenty-foot granite monument which marks the place occupied by these guns to mark the place from which the death-dealing shot and shell were hurled that resulted in the death of so many of Kentucky's noble and brave boys.

I understand this monument was erected by the president of one of the great railway systems, the N.C.& St. L., who had participated in the famous charge. It is the most interesting and historic point of all the very interesting points of this eventful field. It was with awe and overpowering wonder and feeling that I indulged the scenes of fifty years ago, enacted on this spot. Here the very earth trembled beneath the thunderings of these fifty-eight cannon, sending death and destruction into the ranks of us poor unfortunate Confederates.

The tablet upon this monument reads as follows:

"On January 2, 1863, at three p.m., there were stationed on this hill, fifty-eight cannon commanding the field across the river and as the Confederates advanced over this field the shot and shell from these guns resulted in a loss of 1,800 killed and wounded in less than one hour."

What a harvest of death in so short a time was wrought by shot and shell! The most of whose victims were mutilated and lacerated beyond recognition or description. Had the earth been torn by an earthquake the scene would not have been more terrible and hideously appalling.

On a board marker, near by, in faded letters is this indefinite inscription:

"Col. S. Mat. —, Third Division 14th A.C.

Fed. —, Col. S. W. Price commanding. Holding Lower Ford, Dec. 31, 1862."

This evidently refers to the battery that played upon Cobb and Slocum on Swain's Hill.

It would seem from these last words of this poster that the Federals were afraid on the first day's fight that the Confederates would attempt to turn their left by crossing at this ford, hence the placing of this battery here. Bragg, it seems, had no such thought, and, however, it was stationed in our immediate front, West from Swain's Hill and as the battle progressed on the plain south of the railroad and turnpike it played upon Cobb and Slocum with increasing vigor and spirit. As before stated, the Orphans were stationed at this time in support to these batteries, and it was from this point that I witnessed the thrilling sights on the west side of the river.

In company with my new-made genial and accommodating friend, W. G. Beatty, whose father owned the land on which the battle of the 2nd was fought, I visited Swain's Hill, which is evidently a mistaken name for the place, no one with whom I conversed, old or young, knew it by that name. I found on the hill, which I very readily recognized from the distance, the old entrenchments intact, save from the leveling effects of time, and on which an occasional locust sapling is growing with quite a thicket of the same in the immediate front. But from the left of this line of works and where I was stationed on the 31st the view overlooking the railroad, turnpike and plain is perfectly clear. From here I looked, studied and wondered. Why should I not linger and contemplate? Never until the great day of judgment do I ever expect to witness such a thrilling and awe-inspiring scene as I here witnessed on that eventful day of December 31, 1862.

Beatty contemplated me with interest, if not astonishment. So intensely interesting were these scenes and recollections I was almost tempted to spend another day contemplating and reviewing them. But we returned to the city at night to attend a church affair at the instance and invitation of my young friend from Bourbon, Rev. Everett Smith, whose guest I had been while here.

I tried hard to forget, and partially succeeded in forgetting, the thoughts and reminiscences the day had suggested in the presence of so many charming ladies and gallant gentlemen of Brother Smith's congregation and the additional enjoyment of the ice cream, cakes and strawberries, my appetite of fifty years ago suddenly returning to remind me of the difference twixt now and then.

Next morning my friend Beatty was on hand early with his automobile and speeded me over the city which I am frank to say is one of the most beautiful little cities I ever saw. I was charmed by the old time warmth and hospitality of its people and the greeting given me and I shall remember them as among the happiest of my life. And if I were young once more, I would be almost tempted to cast my lot with these good people in this good country, both of which are the next best to Kentucky.

I must not forget to remind the old Orphans and others who may read this paper that after considerable inquiry I was able to find the old Haynes home, in which General Hanson died, and which is now occupied by Hon. Jesse C. Beasley, the present Democratic nominee for Congress in this district. I was shown through the house by his good little wife who, although taken somewhat by surprise at my sudden and unexpected visit, courteously invited me to examine and inspect until fully satisfied. I stood in the room in which he died almost dumfounded with emotion. Here, in the presence of his heart-broken wife, and sorrowing friends, his life gradually ebbed away and took its flight to the realms above.

I was reminded to tread lightly and speak softly on this solemn occasion, for here passed away into the Great Beyond one of Kentucky's grandest and greatest noblemen.

I attended that afternoon, in company with Captain Baird, Beatty and others, the anniversary decoration of the Confederate graves and listened to a fine oration and the delightful rendering of several appropriate songs by the Murfreesboro quartette. When they sang "My Old Kentucky Home," I hugged tightly the tree against which I leaned and fear I betrayed a weakness for which I am not altogether ashamed – for what Kentuckian that lives, especially when away from home, whose soul is not moved when he hears the sweet strains of this touching and soul inspiring song. How can he, when thus

reminded of his old Kentucky home, keep from ex-
claiming (in mind at least) in the language of the
poet:

Lives there a man (Kentuckian) with soul so dead,
Who to himself hath not said,
This is my own, my native land.

Before closing this chapter I must not fail to
say that I found on this trip a manifestation of the
same liberal hospitable and magnanimous spirit that
has ever characterized this noble and self-sacrificing
people. To the good women of the South I owe my
life; to them I bow and acknowledge obeisance as
the truest, purest, sweetest and best of all God's
creatures.

No sacrifice that mortal man could make is
too great a recompense for the love and devotion of
these dear women who sacrificed, wept and suffered
during the four long years of midnight darkness.
They are the angels of the earth today; to them as
such I uncover my head and I hail them.

Finally I wish to acknowledge my thanks to
Mr. and Mrs. C. D. Ivie, at whose home I was the
guest of my friend, Rev. Smith and his charming
little wife. To Editor Williams, W. G. Beatty, Cap-
tains Baird and Mitchell, Dr. Campbell and others,
I am indebted for many courtesies and favors.

CHAPTER SIX

☆ ☆ ☆ ☆

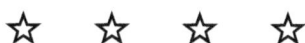

Lookout Mountain.
Battle of Chickamauga – 1863

I am now attempting to write from this Lookout Mountain, one of the most picturesque as well as interesting places on the American continent. Near by and round about here some of the greatest episodes in the world's history transpired near the close of that eventful year, 1863.

Chickamauga, Lookout Mountain, Missionary Ridge, where the lives of sixty-five thousand Americans were either destroyed or more or less wrecked.

A feeling of philosophy and awe prompts me to ask why all this great sacrifice of human life, misery and suffering?

Was the Great God that made man now looking on this awful scene of carnage and woe again repenting that He had made wicked, rebellious and murderous man; or was it a part of His omnipotent plan for man's inherent folly and wickedness driving him to destroy his fellowman? Whatever it was it seems to have been accomplished here amid these towering mountains.

But so it was and I, one insignificant actor in the grand drama, am still permitted to live and re-count some of the thrilling scenes as they were en-acted. It is beyond my power to describe minutely and correctly all the thrilling sights that I witnessed on this eventful occasion (Battle of Chickamauga) and I shall refer to those only that concern myself and my Kentucky comrades, unless incidentally it shall appear necessary to my story.

I will, therefore, not attempt to note the ma-neuvering, the marching and counter-marching, back and forth, up and down the Chickamauga Valley, in and about Rossville and Crawfish Springs and their vicinity; all of which, at that time, seemed to me was but the waving of the red flag in the face of Rosecrans in "I dare you to come out" spirit on the part of Bragg.

Whatever motives, schemes and strategy it contained, we all knew, rank and file, field and staff, that we were on the eve of momentous events. We all knew that here the question of "Greek meeting Greek" would soon again be tested and two of the mightiest armies of modern times would be locked in mortal combat. We had not long to wait, for on the morning of the nineteenth (September, 1863), an occasional boom, boom, away to the right and front told us of the coming storm that was about to break over and sweep Chickamauga Valley with a mighty avalanche of thunder and horror that shook the very earth itself. Slowly but steadily the roar of artillery increased and by the middle of the afternoon became almost incessant.

Longstreet's Virginians had come out to show the Western army how to fight and they were now learning that Rosecrans' Western veterans could give instructions in the art of war as well as they, and that they were not facing the aliens and wage soldiers that constituted a large part of the Army of the Potomac. They also found, as the battle progressed, that the Western army of the South knew as well and were as willing to "stand up Johnnie" and give and take blow for blow as they. The evening wore on and occasional reports from the front brought news that the Confederates were holding their own and a little better.

Meantime the "Orphans" were on the move toward the front and facing the enemy's moving column on the Chattanooga road, which led to Rossville and near Glass' Mill, at which place the artillery of Breckinridge's division, commanded by the gallant Major Graves, engaged the enemies in one of the fiercest artillery duels it was my pleasure to witness during the war. I say pleasure advisedly, for it was a magnificent sight to see from where I was stationed Graves moving among his men and directing their every action, which was done with an admirable celerity and precision that was perfectly charming. I must here do Graves the honor to say that he was the most perfect military man I ever saw. But this was but the prelude to the play of the morrow; both parties seeming (after a half hour's engagement) to say we will settle tomorrow. "Sunday is a better day."

Shifting our position to Lee and Gordon's Mill, further down the Chickamauga, in the afternoon, we here awaited developments and that night made a long detour and crossed at Alexander's Bridge, several miles down the river. Next morning we found ourselves on the extreme right of the dividing line of the stage of action marked out by the respective commanders for the grand tragedy that day to be enacted upon the stage of war. Early, very early, the Fourth Kentucky Skirmishers (and I here glory in the fact) had the honor of firing the first shots in the opening that day of the greatest battle ever fought on the American continent, if not the greatest in modern times. This assertion may be called in question by critics, but if I mistake not there were more men killed and wounded at Chickamauga than in any other engagement of the war.

Here the old and somewhat sacrilegious saying of "hell broke loose in Georgia" was fully and forcefully emphasized by the almost continuous thundering of 200 cannons that made the very earth tremble, besides the constant rattle of musketry and the shouts of more than a hundred thousand struggling combatants determined on each other's destruction. Americans all, and all for what? That a God-made inferior race might occupy the same plane with the superior was the object of one, while that right was disputed by the other. But I fear I may be digressing somewhat from the original purpose in these chapters. Still these thoughts are hard to suppress. Reviewing the incidents of the great battle and the part played by Kentucky Confederates I return to the skirmish line of the Fourth Kentucky, which covered the front of the Orphan Brigade and which was commanded by Col. Joe Nuckols, who was wounded at the very outset of the engagement and compelled to leave the field.

The writer was the subject at this particular time and place of the most ridiculous and practical joke of his entire war experience, but which (thanks to the Bill of Rights) he is not here compelled to relate. This was the beginning of that chapter in the history of the Orphan Brigade, which took the lives and blood of so many noble Kentuckians to write. In the first and desperate onset, led by the noble and intrepid Helm, whose name is a household word with almost all Kentuckians, fell here, together with Graves, Hewitt, Dedman, Daniel, Maderia and other officers of the line, and many splendid men of the Second and Ninth Regiments, who paid with their lives tribute to Mars and added to Kentucky's old traditional glory and renown.

Three regiments on the right – Fourth, Sixth and Forty-First Alabama – swept everything before them – the enemy being in the open field. But the Second and Ninth encountered the enemies' breastworks and were repulsed with terrible slaughter. Here was where the officers just mentioned fell in one of the most desperate struggles of the day. Here "Pap Thomas'" veterans took advantage of their works and exacted deep and merciless toll. More than once during the day was this position assailed by other bodies of Confederates with similar results. About the middle of the afternoon the assembling of Cheatham's and Walker's division in conjunction with Breckinridge warned us that the fatal moment had arrived and the hour of desperation was at hand.

The old veteran needs no one to tell him when a crisis is approaching. He instinctively and otherwise comprehends the meaning of these movements and nerves himself for the desperate work before him. His countenance would convince the stoic of what his mind contained; in modern parlance, he "understands the game." When the signal gun was fired we knew its meaning, so also did the enemy. Then three lines in solid phalanx, desperate and determined men, moved forward on the Federal stronghold to be met by a withering and blighting fire from the enemy behind their works. But so furious and desperate was the onslaught that Thomas' veterans, who had withstood all previous attempts to dislodge them, could no longer face the line of gleaming bayonets of the Confederates as they leaped over the breastworks the Federals had so successfully defended up to that hour.

Some surrendered, others made their escape and still others met their doom – many, not hearing the shouts of the victorious Confederates as they rushed over and among them.

This was the culmination of the struggle. Similar movements with similar results were taking place simultaneously all along the line, closing the most stupendous struggle of the war. But at this particular point and at Snodgrass Hill, where the Fifth Kentucky contributed additional and unsurpassed glory to Kentucky's part in the great battle, were the keys to Rosecrans' position, and here the fighting was the hardest and the losses heaviest.

In the first charge in the morning where the right of the brigade was so successful, we captured a section of the enemy's artillery. The writer seized the trunnion of one of the guns and with assistance turned it on them, while the other was turned by others of our men; but we could find no ammunition to fire them and were deprived of the anticipated glory of firing on the enemy as they fled from the field. I wish here, and in my feeble way, to lift my hat to do honor to the gallantry of the captain commanding that battery (who I learned was from Indiana) as doing the most daring and chivalrous act I ever saw performed by an enemy during my entire war experience. Both his lieutenants and a number of his men having been killed before he abandoned his guns, which were in a battery just on the west side of the Chickamauga road and in the face of us Confederates, who had reached the east side of the road, he dashed into the road and past us, lifting his hat and waving us a salute that would have put to shame a Chesterfield or a Prince Rupert. The act was almost paralyzing and not a man of the fifty or more who fired at him point blank touched him or his horse. If there is such a thing as a charmed life, this captain must have possessed it on that occasion. If living I would gladly travel miles to shake his hand.

Our next move was to unite our separated line which we did by retiring later on to the point from where we started.

During the occasional lulls in the musketry firing, the artillery from left to right and especially on the left about Snodgrass Hill was thundering defiance and sending death into each other's ranks that seemingly made old earth shake from center to circumference, set the birds to flight, caused reptiles, lizards and all manner of wild animals to flee from the wrath of murderous man, among which was a cotton-tail deer that was seen by some of the men running in a bewildered and dazed manner in the rear of the contending lines, not knowing which way to flee or what it all meant.

The enemy routed, the conflict ceased – about dark – with the Orphans (those left) on the west side of the Chickamauga road, some of the men playfully astride the enemy's guns – several in number – that had been abandoned at this point, others prostrate on the ground resting and recounting incidents of the day – ALL glad enough that it was over.

Here General Buckner rode up, he having come over from the left where his artillery and division of infantry had done such splendid work and who was greeted with a cheer from the surviving

Orphans that must have done his soul good and which he acknowledged with a smile, lifting his hat gracefully in acknowledgment of the greeting.

What next! We all expected that we would follow immediately without an hour's delay on the heels of the retreating and discomfited Federals and overtake and completely rout and possibly capture them before they could get settled behind their fortifications around Chattanooga. But here the fatal mistake of Beauregard at Shiloh (and for which Bragg censured him) was duplicated by Bragg himself.

Back to the field among the boys where we spent the night among the dead and wounded; and awaiting orders from Bragg, who was spending his time in sending congratulations to President Davis while Rosecrans was busy preparing to receive and entertain him from his fortifications around Chattanooga.

The writer having learned that we would likely spend the day on the field resting – "resting" (I toss my head in derision of the thought), – obtained permission to visit and inspect the field of battle, and in company with one or two comrades started early next morning from the extreme right, where we opened the battle, and traversed the entire length of the field, a distance of seven miles or more. This was the first time such an enviable opportunity had ever presented itself and I seized it gladly, notwithstanding the many horrible and ghastly sights I knew I would see. On every hand, in every direction, were evidences of the desperate conflict of the preceding day. The forest trees splintered and torn by the plunging shot and shell from the cannon's deadly throat, dismantled caissons and artillery wheels, dead horses, guns, cartridge boxes, bayonets and almost every kind of war paraphernalia imaginable were strewn promiscuously over the field. Trees and saplings, not larger than a man's body to a height of six or eight feet, contained from a dozen to as high as sixty rifle balls. But worst of all with upturned faces and glaring eyes, torn and mangled bodies of not less than four thousand dead men on the field and at the hospitals. At the latter, especially at the Snodgrass place, there were acres covered with wounded and many dead. Here I witnessed the most appalling sight my eyes ever beheld, a description from which I shudder and shrink at this distant day, and which is too terrible for delicate and sensitive natures to ponder; and which involuntarily reminds me of Sherman's saying again. The citizens of today will doubtless wonder how any man could escape such a rain of shot and shell, but by the old soldier it is readily understood. While ninety per cent of these shots were being fired the men were lying flat on their faces and were overshooting each other when suddenly one or the other would spring to his feet and with a bound and a yell rush at a double-quick upon their foe, giving him time to fire one or at most two rounds when his ranks would be broken and compelled to retire.

After seeing these appalling sights I retraced my steps and reached the starting point about twilight to find that my command had been ordered forward toward Chattanooga and the vicinity of Missionary Ridge, which we reached next day to find Rosecrans occupying his fortifications and redoubts ready to receive and entertain us. We were formed in line of battle at or near the foot of Missionary Ridge and expected when the formation was completed to be hurled against the forts and redoubts to certain and inevitable destruction.

Many expressions of evil and forebodings of disaster were indulged in and anathemas were hurled at the commander without stint for holding us back for this, the hour of our doom. Many farewells were being exchanged, mingled with jeers and sarcasm, all knowing and understanding fully the gravity of the situation. It was an hour of intense, of dreadful suspense, which could only be felt and not described.

But thanks to an all wise and merciful Providence which at the last moment withheld the hand and changed the mind that commanded. But for this change of mind he who writes this story would doubtless now be "sleeping the sleep that knows no waking on fame's eternal camping ground." When we were ordered to retire to Missionary Ridge many were the long drawn sighs of relief that we had escaped from this threatened and, as we felt, certain doom.

A Visit to Chickamauga in May, 1912

I have visited scenes of the great conflict twice, traversed the very ground from the point where we

formed line of battle and moved to the charge
against "Pap" Thomas' veterans and am still unsatis-
fied. Not that the points of greatest interest have
been lost to memory, but because memory will not
be satisfied. I can see in my mind the anxious look
in the faces of those brave Kentucky boys, as they
stepped into line and touched elbows in obedience
to the commands "dress to the right; dress to the left;
steady, steady, men; quick step, forward, march!"

Tell me I shall ever forget these commands or
this hour! Never, while "memory lasts and reason
holds sway."

From this very starting point I traced the
ground over which we moved (in 1863) taking the
monument erected to the memory of General Helm
as a guide and allowing for the space of the two regiments to occupy the right, coursing westward, the
exact direction we moved, crossing the LaFayette
road at or near the very point where the two pieces
of artillery were captured and previously referred to.
The tablet here tells me who my gallant captain of
Indiana (Bridges) was and recites the facts of the
capture correctly. There, too, is the open field
through which the broken regiments of infantry were
fleeing that I was so anxious to assist with shots
from their own battery.

Here I must criticise a little at the risk of cen-
sure. I will do so by quoting from memory, not literally, from Gen. Breckinridge's official report, saying, "That a strong supporting line at this moment,
thrown on Thomas' flank and rear, would have re-

sulted in dislodging and overthrowing Thomas early in the day." This was plain to line and field officer alike. The opportunity was presented but not availed of; why, I know not.

The tablets here, with their historic record briefly stamped in metal, are substantially correct. My version of the battle previously stated to the guides while going out (I. P. Thoeford, an old Confederate and S. P. Black) was so nearly identical that these men threw up their hands in amazement when I read from the tablet. It was no trouble to convince them that I had been there and knew something about the battle and the positions of the troops on that part of the line. Here stands nearby the Glenn House, some old log houses. Not far away is the Kentucky monument, a fitting memorial to Kentuckians of both sides crowned with the Goddess of Love and Peace. Northeast is the monument to that gallant, lovable character, Ben Hardin Helm – my hand trembles as I write his name, for I really believe he was one of the kindest-hearted and best men I ever knew. Near this spot was where so many of the Second and Ninth fell, some of whose names are already mentioned in this chapter on Chickamauga. I could write much, very much, more of this very interesting and historic field, but will not trespass further on your time and space.

CHAPTER SEVEN

☆ ☆ ☆ ☆

Missionary Ridge. Kentucky Confederate Visits Scenes of Battle and Siege During Civil War

From here (Missionary Ridge) about the last of September the Orphans were sent to Tyner Station as a base from which to guard the commissary stores at Chickamauga Station, that place being the depot of supplies for the army investing Chattanooga.

But when it was seen that Grant, who had arrived and assumed command of the Federal Army, was planning to move on our lines on Lookout and Missionary Ridge, we were ordered back to our original position on the Ridge, not far from Bragg's headquarters. From this point we could see on the night of the 24th of November the flashes from the rifles of the contending lines on Lookout, like so many fireflies on a hot July evening.

The extravagant talk about Hooker's "battle above the clouds" is a misnomer that has found its way into print, and for a long time filled the papers and magazines and is nothing but a magnified myth (unsupported by facts) that is absolutely incredible. At no time were the contending forces more than half way up the mountain, and all the glory arrogated by the Federals was achieved over a light line deployed as skirmishers, composed of Alabamans. For a long time this twaddle was absolutely and positively sickening.

But I must return to my beloved Orphans. Next morning (25th) before daylight we were ordered to the extreme right (northern point of the Ridge) as support to Cleburne's division, a man who was never known to ask for support. This move was a complete waste of that important element of strength at this critical and all-important time, for we, the Orphans, rendered practically no service at all on that eventful day. But here I conjecture and philosophize again. May be and perhaps it was providential, for had we kept our place in the line between and among Cobb's guns, "Lady Breckinridge," "Lady Buckner" and "Lady Helm," and his other guns to which the Orphans were lovingly endeared, they would never have been surrendered while a man was on his feet. Lucky indeed for Sheridan and Wood that day that the Orphans were away from home, and perhaps equally lucky for some, if not all, of us, for we had sworn never to abandon this position while a man of us lived.

This, in my mind, was the strongest natural position with one exception (Rockyface Gap) ever held by the Confederate forces in the West, and its abandonment was a disgrace to Confederate arms. Imagine our mortification and deep chagrin when we learned that our battery – Cobb's – with the endearing names inscribed thereon, had been cowardly abandoned after we had successfully defended them at Shiloh, Vicksburg, Baton Rouge, Murfreesboro, Jackson, Chickamauga and other places. It was enough to make an angel weep and justified the anathemas hurled at the commander and the cowardly troops that were left to defend them. The circumstance left a sting that never can be forgotten while an Orphan survives.

We never knew what had happened until about dark, when we were ordered from our position toward Chickamauga Station. Then the truth took first the form of conjecture, then misgiving and lastly the sad news that we were to cover the retreat of the army. Then all was explained.

The retreat that night was one of intense hardship and excitement, and it was entrusted to the Orphan Brigade, with the help of Cleburne's division, to protect the retreating army. We were in their grasp had they only known it. Passing so near one of their pursuing columns we could actually hear them talking and see them moving around the camp fires they were kindling. To prevent being ambushed we threw out a string of guards on both sides of the road, who moved along parallel with the road and near it. Every moment we expected an attack.

The feeling was one of intenseness and we

were greatly relieved when at last we became assured of our escape.

Had the Federals only known it, they had our retreating column cut in two and could have made a finish of the day's work and probably the Confederacy as well.

But they, too, as well as the Confederates, failed sometimes to grasp their opportunities. One of the pleasant and enjoyable features of this night's experience was the wading of Chickamauga River, waist deep, which had a tendency to further exasperate us and cause the men to express themselves in anything but Sunday school phrase and song.

Next day was but little less exciting. The Federal advance was pressing us with unusual vigor and compelled us to turn time and again from the line of march and check their advance. It was fight and run until Cleburne determined to, and did, put an end to it, ambushing them at Ringgold Gap, where they paid for their persistence with the lives of several hundred men.

After this costly warning from Cleburne we were permitted to continue our retreat unmolested and reached, the next day, that haven of rest, Dalton, about which I have written in a subsequent chapter.

I am making my chapter on Mission Ridge short because there is nothing pertaining to it that is to the credit of the Confederate soldier as a whole. Yet there were some commands of the army that did their duty well and creditably.

In looking at the tablets of many – in fact most

of the Federal regiments and brigades which contain a summary of their losses – I was struck with amazement at the very light loss sustained in this memorable engagement, so disgraceful to the Confederates. Some regiments losing only one man killed and ten or twelve wounded, and no brigade, so far as I noticed, lost more than thirteen men, which was an average of three to the regiment. We had a single company, Company I, of the Fourth Kentucky, that lost more men at Shiloh than a whole brigade here.

When considering the great advantage of position held by them and the insignificant losses inflicted upon the Federals, the losses but emphasize the fact that the Confederates must have been badly rattled on this summit and would no doubt have made a better fight from their entrenchments at the base of the mountain bordering the valley, over which the columns of Grant moved to the attack.

But let us think and reason for the moment, and if possible find some excuse for this miserable failure. It is well known to the expert marksman and sportsman as well, that in shooting on a steep decline you are much more apt to overshoot than when directing a shot horizontally or upward. This was the case there on these steep mountain sides, which furnishes the one excuse only for such bad marksmanship and the low per cent of casualties just noticed. But notwithstanding this fact, a much more creditable record could have been made by rolling the huge boulders that were abundant down upon the Federals, whose progress was, of course, necessarily slow; and, lastly, when the enemy reached the summit exhausted, what were their bayonets for and why did they not use them? These are questions that suggest themselves to the mind of the writer at this distant day, while looking at this natural and seeming impregnable position. As stated before, the history on one part of the field would have been differently written had not the Orphans been taken away from their pets – "Lady Buckner," "Lady Breckinridge," "Lady Helm," "Lady Hanson," "Lady Lyon" and others of their companions in war. A feeling of chagrin creeps over me when I think of the surrender of these guns with their endearing names and hitherto immortal history.

But General Bragg, in his wisdom – no, his unwisdom – thought it best to send us away from our idols and hazard them in the keeping of those who betrayed their trust, and left us, like Rachael, weeping, because they were lost and we "also refused to be comforted."

I find almost innumerable tablets, markers and monuments placed here to commemorate the deeds of valor here performed by the Federals; but I find very few (which is well) to mark the Confederates and their deeds. But could I have my way every one of these would be removed and in their stead I would place the Goddess of Liberty, weeping for shame that her children had so dishonored their heritage.

I have said that I would be brief, and choking back the feeling of remorse and disgrace that this one incident in the history of the Confederate soldier has fixed upon their otherwise brilliant and incomparable record, I close by referring the reader to Murfrees-boro.

CHAPTER EIGHT

☆　☆　☆　☆

Dalton

Who that spent the winter of '63-'64 at Dalton does not recall some circumstance or incident to remind him of the dreary "winter of discontent" spent in this mountain fastness of Northern Georgia? To many of us it seemed like an age, but withal it was a season of much needed rest and recuperation. Here in and around this little city flanked by majestic mountains, pondering over the disasters of Lookout and Missionary Ridge, we spent the time in comparative comfort and ease, some planning in mind the future campaign and its outcome, others indifferent as to the future and caring but little, willing to entrust all to those at the helm, and making the most of circumstances and the ever present, little thinking or caring for the great dangers and hardships that awaited us.

There was from the time we turned our faces southward from Bowling Green to the very close of the war an air of indifference, a "devil may care," happy-go-lucky spirit, about these young Kentuckians that made them ready to cheerfully undertake any enterprise, no matter how dangerous or exacting the duty or perilous the undertaking. They had become so accustomed to all these things, and so thoroughly inured to hardships, that they felt themselves prepared for and rather coveted them, no matter how great or trying. While here we enjoyed more liberty and recreation than any time during or since the war began. Some of the men were furloughed and enjoyed a few days of rest with relatives and friends (if perchance they had any) in the South. The writer spent his in gay old Richmond on the James, in company with General Lewis, Captain McKendrie and other Kentuckians there assembled. All amused themselves as best they could in camp and town.

Drilling had been dispensed with – no need now for that, for in this we were perfect. Dress parade, guard mount and review were about the only exercises now required. A great sham battle broke the monotony once, and a snowball battle at another time was a diversion indulged for one day. A very pertinent question was often asked toward the close of the winter – "Who would command in the next campaign?" When at last it was given out that General Johnson would command, the spirits of the men revived and hope was again renewed. While contemplating the future, news came that the enemy were now moving Daltonward. We indulged the hope and wondered whether Sherman would undertake to force the pass in Rockyface Mountain through which the railroad and wagon road both ran. We thought of Leonidas and his Spartans and hoped for an opportunity to imitate and if possible to eclipse that immortal event at Thermopylæ. But not so the wily Sherman. That "old fox" was too cunning to be caught in that or any other trap.

We were ordered out to meet him and took position in the gap and on the mountain, from which we could see extending for miles his grand encampment of infantry and artillery, the stars and stripes floating from every regimental brigade, division and corps headquarters and presenting the greatest panorama I ever beheld. Softly and sweetly the music from their bands as they played the national airs wafted up and over the summit of the mountain. Somehow, some way, in some inexplicable and unseen manner, "Hail Columbia," "America" and "The Star Spangled Banner" sounded sweeter than I had ever before heard them, and filled my soul with feelings that I could not describe or forget. It haunted me for days, but never shook my loyalty to the Stars and Bars or relaxed my efforts in behalf of our cause.

While thus arrayed in his grand encampment, his banners flying and bands playing, a part of his force (McPherson's Corps), like a gladiator, was rapidly and stealthily gliding over the plain west of the mountains to seize Snake Creek and Dug Gaps and strike Johnson in the rear at Resaca. But you know "the best laid schemes of mice and men gang aft agley." We arrived there first and gave him a hearty welcome, as described in my chapter on Resaca.

Dalton, like other towns and cities, has changed wonderfully in the days since the war. From a quaint old mountain town of a half century ago to the modern and thrifty little city of today, putting on airs like many other towns. To me no landmarks are visible save the old stone springhouse, near where General Lewis had his headquarters and Captain Phillips, A.Q.M. of the Fourth, had his quartermaster store and where his lovely little wife graced his "marquee" with the air and dignity of the queen that she was. I walked over the ground on which the Fourth was encamped and stood upon the very spot where Captain Hugh Henry's tent was pitched, and in which we were often entertained by the Kentucky Glee Club, which was composed of some of the finest talent in the army. While it may not be altogether relevant to the purpose of these chapters, I cannot refrain from referring to and mentioning the fact that the Fourth Kentucky was admitted to have the finest band in the Western Army, led by that accomplished and expert musician who (after the war) became a teacher in the Boston Conservatory of Music – Billy McQuown. Many, many times were we regaled by the music of our band and carried back to the bosom of friends by the sweet strains of "My Old Kentucky Home" and other familiar and inspiring airs played by this band. It is no stranger, than it is true, that music exercises a wonderful and inspiring influence over the soldier, making him forget the hardships, trials and dangers to which he is almost constantly exposed, and troops are never happier than when being entertained in this way, unless it be at a full mess table.

I have been reluctantly compelled to pass by Kennesaw and Pine Mountains, both of which are places of much interest to surviving Orphans. On the former we left several of our best officers and men. Among the former was Major John Bird Rogers of the Fourth Kentucky Regiment, and Lieutenant Bob Innis of the Second. Than the former there was not a more capable and gallant officer identified with the history of the Orphan Brigade as was also Lieutenant Innis.

Pine Mountain, a lone sentinel of nature, was made sacredly historic by the blood of the great preacher, General Bishop Polk. I saw the "grand old man" as he, Generals Johnston and Bates and others rode by the Orphans' position to the summit of the mountain to view and examine the enemy's position in front, and could not but admire the graceful and dignified bearing of the grand old man as he saluted in true military style as he passed. I saw the smoke from and heard the thunder of Simonson's guns as they sent the fatal shot that tore his body and ended his earthly career. Sad and awful moment for the Confederacy! But we have here presented one of the most noted and conspicuous characters in America history. I stood on the very spot on which he fell not twenty minutes after the sad occurrence – Burton's sharpshooters with their Kerr rifles having driven Simonson and his gunners to cover. I believe the sacred spot should have erected on it a monument commemorative of this tragic incident and the life and character of this great man. It is certainly a picturesque and interesting spot.

But before I go I must tell of my visit to Rockyface Gap. Here is one of the grand sentinels of nature – a lofty and stone-crowned mountain towering above and looking contemplatively down upon his neighbors and the low-bending valleys upon whose bosom Sherman pitched his grand and imposing encampment in the make-believe that he was going south through this impregnable pass held by Johnson. Next to Lookout it is the grandest mountain in the Appalachian chain, and one well worthy of a visit by the tourist lover of nature. I climbed to the top of it this morning, going over the same identical path traveled by us while doing picket and observation duty. Here we had the only human telegraph line I ever saw, which was made by placing the operator (an officer) on the summit to report the operations and movements of the enemy to the first man in the line, he repeating it to the next in line and so on down the mountain to its base where the general had his staff officers and couriers to receive the message and report to him at his headquarters. The scheme worked like a charm, notwithstanding its uniqueness.

I was impelled to make this trip – although I felt when I reached the summit I was about to collapse – to see the resting place of a noble and brave old Orphan who was killed while on duty here – George Disney of Company K, Fourth Kentucky – an account of whose singular death is noted by Virginius Hutchings in the history of the Orphan Brigade. I learned before going on this trip that the Boy Scouts of Dalton, under Captain Sapp, county clerk, had only two days before gone up and placed a marble headstone to the grave to take the place of the board that had so long marked his resting place – a place that a monarch or king might envy, hundreds of feet above common man.

I wished while there, so high upward toward heaven, that I could wield the pen of a Gray or a Kipling, that I might do this subject of my thoughts justice. The subject, the inspiration, was here, but language to express it was lacking. Poor George! You have had one friend after these long years to leave a tear of tribute to your memory.

I cannot close without first thanking the good daughters of Dalton for the compliment they paid me by really forcing upon me undeserved attentions in a very fine lunch set before and out of time specially for me just before taking the train at 11:50 a.m., and who I think had a scheme to force me to make them a speech – it being Decoration Day – but I slipped through their fingers and got away.

CHAPTER NINE

☆   ☆   ☆   ☆

Visit to Resaca – 1912.

May 14th found us after a tiresome night's march at Resaca, from which point I again write you.

Here today and on the morrow was fought the first battle of magnitude in the great hundred and twenty days' battle of the celebrated Georgia campaign from Dalton to Atlanta. I say hundred and twenty days' battle, which may seem a little far-fetched, but which is almost literally true, for there was not a day or night, yes scarcely an hour, that we did not hear the crack of a rifle or roar of a cannon. Their sounds were our lullaby, sleeping or waking – to their music we slept, by their thunderings we were awakened, and to the accompanying call of the bugle we responded on the morning of May 14 to engage in the death grapple with Sherman's well clothed, well fed and thoroughly rested veterans – a matter "of Greek meeting Greek" again. Sherman had pushed down the west side of Rockyface Mountain and through Snake Creek Gap the day and night before in an effort to cut Johnston's communications and take him in the rear. But we had been doing some marching and digging, too, and when Sherman's columns four or five deep debouched from their positions – a long, heavily wooded ridge – into the narrow valley, on the east side of which we had constructed rifle pits, he found us ready to receive his gay and awe-inspiring columns, who moved in perfect step, with banners flying and bands playing, as though he expected to charm us.

The eagerness of our own men could scarcely be restrained until they had reached the point to which our orders had been given, seventy-five to eighty yards, when our lines opened almost simultaneously a deadly and murderous fire from both infantry and double-shotted artillery, that flesh and blood could not withstand. Retiring in disorder to their original position in the woods, they rallied and reformed, while their artillery was busy playing upon our batteries, from which they received no response whatever – a mystery at the time to many of us, but which we understood a little later on when they again moved down to the attack, to be met in the same manner with both infantry and artillery, and with similar results. Three times during the morning and early afternoon were these attacks made upon our lines, with the same results. It was a veritable picnic for the Confederates and was the second time in the history of the war, up to this time, that we had presented such a glorious opportunity, protected as we were by earthworks, with clear and open ground in front. Had Sherman continued this business during the entire day (as we hoped he would) the campaign would have ended right here, as we had not called into requisition any of our reserve force. The principal part of the afternoon was spent by the artillery – after the infantry had gotten enough of it – on both sides pounding away at each other in a lively and entertaining fashion.

Some daring and courageous deeds were performed by the Federal officers and men on this occasion, the recollection of which is refreshing and exhilarating to the writer, but for want of time I shall be compelled to pass over. However, one instance I will relate as being somewhat interesting to Kentuckians as showing the home spirit and natural feeling existing between them as Kentuckians, although now engaged in the deadly breach. That night some of our boys of the Fourth Kentucky learned from inquiry of our "friends" in our front that we were confronting the Federal Fourth Kentucky (Colonel Tom Croxton), whereupon a bantering of epithets and compliments was at once begun and exchanged in a very amusing and interesting way. I listened to the colloquy with great interest and amusement, which was conducted on our side by Lieutenant Horace Watts, who was a noted wit and humorist. But I regret that I have forgotten the name of his interrogator, whom I recall, however, was from Vanceburg, Ky.

That night was spent in strengthening our

works and preparing for the work of the morrow, which work we well knew was coming. When morning came the appearance of Old Sol was greeted with a signal from a battery immediately in our front, which had been stationed there during the night and protected by substantial and elaborate earthworks. The shots from this battery were directed against Hotchkiss' battalion of artillery, and which the Fourth Kentucky Infantry was supporting. The enemy's guns from every part of the line kept up a continuous fire throughout the entire day and was the greatest open field bombardment of the war. We were much amused at the manner of firing of the battery in our front, which was done by bugle signal, the meaning of which our men soon learned, for a moment later our works would be pierced by their shells and when they exploded threw high in the air a cloud of dirt and smoke from the embankment that almost covered us up. At intervals of about every five or ten minutes the bugle's "whe-whee-deedle-dee-dee" told us of the crash that was coming and almost lifted our scalps and rendered some of us deaf for weeks. Had the day been an hour longer we would have been compelled to abandon our works, for the embankments were almost leveled and the trenches filled.

Two of Hotchkiss' guns were cut down and had to be abandoned, and but for the fact that they had been run back beyond the crest, not a splinter of them would have been left.

Our batteries did not fire a gun that day, having been ordered to withhold their fire in anticipation of another attack by the enemy's infantry. This day's work was a very clever ruse of Sherman's and demonstrated the cunning of that wily general, for while he was thus entertaining us with the main part of his army, especially his artillery, like the sly old fox that he was, he was planning our undoing by sending down the river to our rear Dodge's Corps to fall on our rear and cut our communications and intercept our retreat.

Had his plan been expedited by Dodge, as it might have been, it would surely have been "all day" with us poor devils of Confederates. It was certainly a "close shave," for which we were all very thankful. But we here on the 14th enjoyed the "picnic" for which we Orphans paid most dearly on the 28th at Dallas, and which I shall describe in another place. War, it seems from my experience and observation, may be described as a dreadful and costly game of "tit-for-tat."

The losses sustained by the Orphans in this engagement at Resaca were insignificant compared with that inflicted upon the enemy in their front. There is not a single recognizable object here save the ground where we fought, from the fact that we arrived here in the night and took our departure in the night. The narrow valley and the long extended ridge in its front and the spur occupied by Hotchkiss and the Fourth Kentucky, is all that I see to remind me of the two days of "pride, pomp and circumstance of glorious war." But how's this, we fighting behind entrenchments and the enemy in the open, four or five lines deep?

"Our loss was 2,747, and his (Johnson's) 2,800. I fought offensively and he defensively, aided by earthwork parapets." – [General Sherman's statement.] There must have been some bad shooting on this occasion – the advantages all on one side, but results so nearly even.

Today, May 16 (1912), marks the forty-eighth anniversary of this important event, and finds me on the ground. Here, as at other places previously mentioned and described, things came back to me and I see them being reenacted. I was accompanied on this inspection by an old comrade (J. H. Norton), who lost an arm at Chancellorsville, and who has lived here in Resaca almost all his life and who was at home at the time, having been discharged on account of the loss of his arm, and who assisted in burying the dead, and he pooh-poohed Sherman's statement as to relative losses. Another old comrade, who is a merchant in the town, told me that he had bought over a hundred thousand pounds of minnie balls picked up on the ground where the battle was fought. I saw a three-bushel box full in his store today. How many poor devils were killed by these would be impossible to tell. They have a neat little cemetery near the town, in which there are nine Kentuckians (Confederates) buried, some of those names I have copied.

CHAPTER TEN

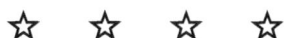

Dallas

Here, as at Balaklava, "some one blundered," and while we have not had a Tennyson to immortalize the event, it is of more than ordinary interest to Kentuckians, especially those who participated in the bloody event – more because of the fearful slaughter and the mournful fact that it was the result of a failure to deliver orders at the proper time. The official report showed a loss of 51 per cent – a loss, considering the time actually engaged, unparalleled in the history of the war. To my mind it was the most desperate and disastrous of all the many engagements in which the Orphans took part during their four years of experience.

The actual time under fire did not in my judgment exceed thirty minutes. To describe accurately the position of the enemy at this distant day would be a difficult task, but it may be said that they occupied two parallel lines of entrenchments, from both of which was delivered simultaneously a destructive and murderous fire so fatal that nothing but the protecting hand of an all-wise and merciful Providence could save. The first of these lines was a few yards below, and in front of the second, which ran along the summit of the ridge and enabled the second line to fire directly overhead without endangering the first. Besides this double advantage, they were able to enfilade our line with their artillery from both extremes of their line. Smith's brigade, on our left, having received orders (which were also intended for us and which failed of delivery) to withhold the attack, enabled the enemy to deliver an oblique fire upon us from his infantry on the left, as well as from his two lines directly in front. At every step Kentucky was paying double toll with the lives of her noblest and best. To push forward meant certain and complete annihilation; to remain where we were, some seventy-five or eighty yards in their front, meant the same, only a little slower death.

The order to "fall back" having been given, we were only too glad to attempt our escape from the death trap into which we had been ordered. Many of our wounded and all of our dead were left on the field or intervening space between the entrenched lines of the opposing forces. Several of the wounded crawled back after nightfall and in this way made their escape. The grounds in the rear of our works presented an appalling sight when I reached them with my burden on my back – Sergeant W.E. Knox, who had a broken leg. Nothing but a miracle saved us both from the murderous fire of the enemy. Here fell the gallant and polished Major Millett within ten paces of our entrenchment, he being the third major of the Fourth Regiment to be killed on the field.

Several incidents of a thrilling and miraculous character occurred on this field, as afterward related. Some of our wounded who approached nearest the enemy's works and fell into their hands were taken to the little town of Dallas, a mile or two distant, where they were found two days later, and left in a shamefully neglected condition. Among them was one of the most noble gentlemen and gallant soldiers it was ever my good fortune to know, Captain D. E. McKendrie of the Sixth Kentucky, and who died a few days later.

There were really only two brigades engaged in this encounter, the Orphan Brigade and Findlay's Florida Brigade. The burden of the encounter fell upon the Orphans, as shown by their greater loss. But here again was displayed that daring, regardless of consequences, which had been so often displayed by this little band of Kentuckians on so many fields from Fort Donelson to this eventful day. I hope I shall not be accused of egotism for seeming to arrogate to myself and my fellow Kentuckians honors to which we are not entitled and of which all of her people may be justly proud. The loss of 51 per cent tells the story more graphically than anything I may say by way of compliment or eulogy.

The reader may wonder why this attack was ordered against a force so strongly and irresistibly posted. The answer is easy to the old veteran who knows the difficulty in ascertaining an enemy's position in a heavily timbered country like this, with trees and bushes in full leaf, and how great the danger from the ever alert sharpshooter to the man attempting a reconnaissance. The object was to develop his strength at this point, the commander believing Sherman to be only feigning while he was carrying out other and ulterior plans. But so it was, we paid dearly for the desired information.

I have reviewed every foot of this ground the second time, stopping here and there to pick up a minnie ball lodged in the enemy's works, fired at them by my dear old "Orphan" boys, and while thus engaged the familiar faces of many a noble comrade and in one or two instances school fellows' images passed before my mind in panorama that almost unnerved and dumfounded me. Studying coolly at this time the great advantage the enemy had in position and numbers, I am surprised that any of us escaped at all. I had no difficulty whatever in locating at once the position of both parties and the exact spot on which my regiment and company fought. Most of the Confederate lines have been partly and in some places completely obliterated by the plow, but hills and hollows are still there. The enemy's lines have been little disturbed and are mostly intact even at this distant day.

I must confess that I am wont to linger about this hallowed spot and my heart beats heavily when I think of the comrades and friends who died here and whose bodies I assisted in giving the last rude sepulchre. I turn away from it with tearful eyes and sorrowful heart.

CHAPTER ELEVEN

☆　☆　☆　☆

Atlanta – May, 1912

I am writing this from historic Atlanta, the "gateway of the South." How very different to the Atlanta I knew in the days gone by when her streets were filled with the tramp, tramp of marching armies, when her walls were rocked by the thunders of the cannon's mighty roar, when the rockets' "red glare gave proof through the night that our new flag was still there." Oh! what a wonderful change 'twixt now and then. "Lovely city now, quiet and mighty in her peaceful ways, may the God of war never again sound his bugle calls over her peaceful slumbers, and may she know the ways of war no more forever."

How very, very different to the Atlanta I saw in June, 1865, when on my way home from the South, returning disabled, discomfited, defeated. What darker picture could be imagined unless it be "Dante's Inferno," than a city of destroyed homes with blackened walls and chimneys punctuating the fiendish spirit that prompted the ruin of its people and their homes. When General Sherman first gave expression to his oft-repeated apothegm he must have had in mind the ruin he had accomplished in the destruction of this fair city of the South. Certainly nothing but a fiendish spirit could have prompted it.

But two buildings of prominence were left – the Masonic Temple and a hotel. But her people are now enjoying the blessings of peace and prosperity, having risen, Phoenix-like, from her ashes.

I must now return to some of the incidents and events of the defense of Atlanta in which I was an humble participant. On the 9th of July General Johnston's army crossed the Chattahoochee River on pontoons and the time until the 22d was employed by Johnston and Hood chiefly in marching and counter-marching to checkmate the movements of Sherman. A circumstance happened about this time that gave Sherman great pleasure (he says so) and correspondingly great sorrow and despondency to the Confederates, heretofore so successfully led by General Johnston, viz., the removal of Johnston and the substitution of Hood.

While Hood was a Kentuckian as well as we Orphans, and we priding in everything pertaining to the history of Kentucky, we had unbounded confidence in General Johnston. But once before had we felt such sadness and regret – when General Breckinridge was taken from us and sent to Virginia. This feeling was intensified by the belief that Bragg was responsible.

On the 20th the battle of Peach Tree Creek was fought and given a prominence in excess of the facts as the writer saw it; a straggling, haphazard kind of hide and seek affair, magnified into a battle. On the 22d of July was fought what is known in history as the battle of Atlanta.

The night march of the 21st from our place in the line of defense on the left and to the extreme right near Decatur, where this battle was fought, was the most trying, with one exception, the writer remembers to have ever experienced, occupying the entire night in dust ankle deep, without a drop of water or an hour's rest. It is remembered to this day with a distinctness that makes me fairly shudder. When morning came we looked like the imaginary Adam "of the earth earthy," so completely were we encased in dust. But for the nerve stimulus that imminent and great danger gives a man on the eve of a great battle, I don't think I could have rendered much service, on this occasion, after such exhaustion and suffering from thirst. In fact were it not an indispensable part of my plan I should have little to say about this whole affair, for it was to me the most ill-conceived and unsatisfactory executed plan of battle of the whole war in which I participated.

There were difficulties to overcome that might easily have been avoided had the proper engineering skill been employed in time and the necessary reconnaissance been made. So far as results accomplished were concerned, it was barren and fruitless. Especially was this the case on the extreme right, where

Bates' division fought and where the Orphans took part. Not that any man or body of men proved recreant, but there was a lack of understanding and cooperation of movement, coupled with almost insurmountable obstacles that might have been avoided. For instance, the Kentucky Brigade was compelled to struggle through the mire of a slough and millpond filled with logs, stumps, brush and what-not in water and mire knee-deep, the men in many instances being compelled to extricate their comrades by pulling them onto logs and other footings before we could pass the obstruction. This so deranged our battle alignment that in the press and excitement of the moment, caused by the enemy firing at this critical moment, we were never able to correct it and present a solid front. Out of dust ankle deep into water and mire knee-deep was too much for the nerves and patience of the strongest man and most patient Christian. And then, to be finally pitched in one disordered and confused mass against a well disciplined and strongly posted line of veterans, behind earthworks, was too much for the best soldiers of the times. And yet with the proper use of artillery at the right time and place, we might have accomplished more decisive results.

This affair was the more lamentable to the Orphans because of the loss of quite a number of our best officers and men without any tangible results. The whole thing was disappointing and to me really disgusting. Hood at Atlanta, like Bragg at Murfreesboro, might profitably have spent more time with his engineers in examining and surveying the ground on which he expected to fight. General Johnson was doubtless better posted. But the final result would have been the same; Atlanta was doomed – by Sherman's force of three to one.

After summing up results and exchanging regrets and expressing sorrow for the loss of comrades, we returned to our original places in the lines of defense to await the next scene in the grand drama. This came on August 6th at Utoy Creek on the Sandtown road leading southwest from Atlanta. The Orphan Brigade and Tyler's Tennessee Brigade had been pushed forward on a kind of salient to the left and front of the main line and touching the little stream known as Utoy Creek. Here occurred the battle known by the above name. I here recognize more distinctly than any other place, so far visited, the general appearance of the ground and especially the falls of the little creek at which on the day previous to the battle I enjoyed the only refreshing bath for several days. It is quite an interesting place to the writer. I here witnessed on the morning of the battle the capture of Lieut. Isham Dudley, in command of the videttes, together with some half dozen men of the Orphan Brigade, they having been completely surprised just at daybreak by a sudden and unexpected rush of the enemy.

The writer had the honor to command the skirmish line covering the Confederate position and had a fine opportunity to witness the charge of the two Federal brigades, which were composed chiefly of East Tennesseans, as they swept past the right of our skirmish line, they doubtless not knowing that they were about to encounter breastworks of a formidable character, receiving at the same time a scathing flank fire from the Fourth Kentucky and the skirmish line above alluded to. But they were plucky fellows and charged to within a few yards of our works, paying dearly for their courage and temerity. In this affair we were attacked by a force somewhat superior in numbers, but the advantage that our breastworks afforded us made the victory easily won. I here quote the order of General S.D. Lee, commanding corps, congratulating them and incidentally complimenting the defenders:

"The lieutenant general commanding takes pleasure in announcing to the officers and men of this corps the splendid conduct of a portion of Bates' Division, particularly Tyler's Brigade and the Second and Fourth Kentucky regiments of Lewis' Brigade, in sustaining and repulsing on yesterday afternoon three assaults of the enemy in which his loss in killed, wounded and prisoners was from eight hundred to a thousand men, with three stands of colors, three or four hundred small arms and all of his entrenching tools. Soldiers who fight with the coolness and determination that these men did will always be victorious over any reasonable number."

In this engagement we lost only about eighteen men all told, while the enemy's loss in killed alone was 160. I walked over the ground ten minutes after it occurred and found the crest of the hill covered with the dead and wounded, swords, guns, cartridge boxes and other paraphernalia of war.

I found here the thing I need and coveted most of all at this time, a fine black sombrero, which furnished me ample protection thereafter from the intense rays of the August sun. I "swapped" my spoon-bill cap with the fellow who had worn this hat, to which he, of course, raised no objection. Others provided themselves in like manner, which was entirely legitimate, of course, the original owners having no further use for such things. But a flanking column that night, as usual, compelled us to abandon the position of our recent victory and we retired to our original position in the circle of entrenchments.

I have this day, May 13, 1912, carefully and studiously reviewed the very spot on which those 160 men lay dead, and I feel safe in saying that it is not larger than one-half a city block. They were met square in front and were fired on from both flanks, and had they attempted to remain there as much as one hour there would not have been a man of them left on his feet. It was a death trap similar to the one into which we Orphans fell at Dallas.

I could hardly control my emotions when viewing this place, and my mind was almost overwhelmed as I walked along on top of these still distinct and undisturbed parapets, stopping now and then to pick up a "Yankee bullet" lodged in them, or a small stone that had been thrown out by the Confederates. The surroundings here are perfectly familiar to me, notwithstanding opinions of friends at home to the contrary. So interesting is this spot that

I have made the second visit to it.

Here the time from August 7 to 29, 1864, was spent in listening to the music of the rifle and the cannon and an occasional sweet, faint and harmonious symphony from the enemy's brass bands as they played, seemingly for our entertainment, "The Star Spangled Banner," "Hail Columbia," "Yankee Doodle" and, to taunt us, "Dixie." At night they would vary the entertainment by sending up innumerable rockets, which some of the men interpreted to mean the arrival of a new command or shift of position, but to most of us it was "Greek and Hebrew."

But this condition was not to last; Sherman's definition of war was in him and must come out. On the 29th we packed our knapsacks and bidding goodbye to the Atlanta of the day, soon to be no more, we again turned southward to meet the flanking columns of Sherman at Jonesboro, with a description of which I shall close these recollections.

Before leaving this dear old city I must take one more last look at her steeples, her walls and her streets, shake the hand of friends in the last farewell grasp and say good-bye forever.

I find Atlanta so wonderfully changed, commercially, assuming metropolitan airs and wearing her honors so gracefully that I dare not attempt a description of her present status. Besides, these things are well known now by the whole American people. Still I find myself comparing her (in mind) with what she was "before and during the war."

The fact that I am now looking upon her for

the last time, and the further fact that she contains many warm and true friends whom I shall never see again, causes a feeling of sadness I wish I could resist. But I break camp and take up my line of march for Jonesboro.

But before I leave I must tender my thanks to my young friend from Bourbon, W.H. Letton (who is now a prosperous business man here), for many favors and courtesies so cheerfully extended me. It were cruel to allow him to spend with me so much of his time from his lovely little Georgia bride, so recently taken to himself. But this is Kentucky, you know, and he inherits it. I am also indebted to my old comrades, J.W. McWilliams of the Forty-Second Georgia; J.M. Mills of the Soldiers' Home, and C.L. Ingram of Fort McPherson; ex-Sheriff Barnes, Major Jones of the Seventeenth Infantry at the fort (McPherson), and last, though not least by any means, Mrs. Jones of the city at whose boarding house I was a guest.

CHAPTER TWELVE

☆   ☆   ☆   ☆

Jonesboro

I begin here the last inspection and reminiscence, on my return trip from attending the recent Confederate reunion at Macon, May, 1912, and while I distrust my ability to do the theme proper justice, I am tempted to undertake the task through the love of the brave "old boys" who still survive and the memory of several hundred noble young Kentuckians whose life blood consecrates the soil of Georgia on every field from Chattanooga to Jonesboro.

My mind becomes a whirlpool of recollections as I stand here and "view the landscape o'er" and contemplate the horrible scenes enacted here forty-eight years ago, and in which the Confederacy was surely and rapidly expiring in the throes of dissolution.

It is not my purpose or aim to controvert in any instance the descriptions and recitals of the historians, but merely as a pastime to revert to some of my personal experiences and recollections. Nor shall I attempt to enlarge upon or embellish the history of that glorious little band of Kentuckians known as the "Orphan Brigade." That has been done by others, done by such men as Prof. N. S. Shaler, Gens. Joseph E. Johnson, W. J. Hardee, Stephen D. Lee, Ed. Porter Thompson and many others, able and eloquent men, historians and statesmen, and in whose history Kentuckians of all beliefs must ever rejoice as one of the brightest and most interesting pages in her history. And why not, since they represented so many of the noblest and best young men of the State and were led by such men as Breckinridge, Hanson, Helm, Lewis, Monroe and others whose names are a synonym of glory and greatness.

When we arrived here (Jonesboro) in the great campaign there were many absent – not without leave, thank God, but with honor, whose brows had been crowned with everlasting wreaths of honor – in death "on Fame's eternal camping ground." When the roll was called no response came from many. Hanson, Helm, Hewitt, Graves, Rogers, Dedman, Madeira, Daniel, McKendrie, Millett, Williams, Innis, Bramblett, Bell and three thousand others failed to answer. But as the "blood of martyrs is the seed of the church," so the sacrifice of these Kentuckians is a diadem in the wreath that encircles her history.

But now I stand on this historic spot where forty-eight years ago the unequal, almost suicidal conflict raged with destruction and fury, and see, in my mind's eye, the raging conflict and hear the cannon's mighty roar, the screaming shot and shell and the ping and whistle of the deadly minnie, the shouts and yells of the combatants as they grapple in the deadly conflict. Here I experienced the pangs of a painful wound from a minnie ball, while assisting a dear friend (Lieutenant Neal), being in the throes of death, both he and the man on my left falling simultaneously. How well I remember the look of anguish upon his noble countenance as he held up both hands, imploring my assistance. Brave, noble fellow and Christian gentleman, I trust and believe his soul rests in peace among the angels.

Imagine my grief on reaching the ambulance (assisted by comrades) to find my bosom friend (and by many said to be my double), Ensign Robert H. Lindsay of Scott County, in the ambulance, he having received a mortal wound from which he died that night while lying upon the same blanket with myself. The reader can imagine my feelings when the dawn of morning came and I threw back the blanket that covered us and beheld his noble countenance cold in death, with the fixed glare of the eyes that told me that my beloved comrade and friend had passed to the realms of eternal glory. Poor Bob! I tried in vain, while on the way to the field hospital, to extort a parting message, a last farewell to mother and family, but the messenger of death held him in his grasp and refused compliance with this last request of his friend who loved him as a brother. A circumstance coincident with his death was the fact that we prepared and ate our dinners together that day, meantime talking over the probable results of the approaching battle and making certain requests of each other in the event that one or the other should fall. Hence my anxiety to hear a last farewell from his dying lips. Memory takes me back over the intervening years and I am tempted to exclaim:

Sing thou music of the spheres
The song of the weeping pines
As the days and years go by,
But let me, Oh! let me not forget,
The dear friend who 'neath them lies.

I have always thought this a singular circumstance, that the three friends – boon companions – holding the same rank, should be stricken down almost at the same moment – that "two should be taken and the one left," but such are the vicissitudes of war.

I can recognize only two landmarks of this historic spot and its surroundings – the old stone depot and the prominent knoll, occupied by the enemy's skirmishers on the morning of the battle (August 31st) and which Lieut. Heck Burden, the commander of that gang of army sleuths, that Sherman and his officers admitted they dreaded – known as the Kentucky sharpshooters – and myself, in a spirit of daring, approached within easy rifle range, by means of a deep gully, and which terminated in one less Federal officer reporting to his commander. I have looked upon this particular spot with no little concern, for it was near this my two dear friends just noted fell, and where I also received my quietus – as a reward, perhaps, for my daring of the morning. This circumstance (my wounding) precludes the mention from personal experience a description of the second day's fight and in which the Orphans sustained the loss of a number of men and officers and resulted in the capture of the greater part of the survivors, Sherman's overwhelming numbers enabling him to outflank and overpower the left of the Confederate line. But they were held as prisoners but a short time and were exchanged and returned to service almost immediately. Here, as in other instances, the enemy outnumbered us three to one and enabled them to envelop our flanks more readily than in previous engagements, the country being without the natural barriers and obstructions that had previously favored us in the mountain section of the country through which we had passed.

Here at Jonesboro ended my service to the Confederacy and my experience as a soldier in the field. The next six months, which brought the war to a close, were spent by me in hospitals, which also came near bringing my earthly career to a close. But, thank God, I am still here and now engaged in reviewing our movements of the past. And I shall be happy if what I may have written should fall under the eye of some old comrade or friend and afford him pleasure or food for contemplation.

APPENDIX

☆ ☆ ☆ ☆

The Organization of the Orphan Brigade
by Thomas D. Osborne, Secretary

The Orphan Brigade, officially styled the First Kentucky Brigade of Infantry, and probably the most famous body of Southern soldiers, was organized in the State of Tennessee. In June, 1861, Gen W. T. Withers, Colonels James W. Hewitt and Robert A. Johnson, backed by wealthy citizens of Louisville, began the work of recruiting soldiers for the South. In July following, Camp Boone, two miles from the L. & N. Railroad and seven miles from Clarksville, was laid off. Young men rallied from all parts of the State and nation. Col. Hewitt resigned from the noted Seventh New York Regiment and came; Capt. Ed. P. Byrne, a Kentucky living in Mississippi, had six brass cannon cast at Memphis and brought them with him to Camp Boone; the Governor of Kentucky marched as a private in the ranks until killed at Shiloh.

Thirty years after the war Prof. Shaler, of

Harvard, in his great articles on "The Natural Man," published in *Scribner's Magazine*, selected the Orphan Brigade as the typical one of the nation, and said: "This was the most purely American command in either army, and was in many respects the most remarkable body of soldiers in the modern world."

The organization of the regiment was as follows: Second Kentucky, Col. Roger W. Hanson; Fourth Kentucky, Col. Robert P. Trabue; Sixth Kentucky, Col Joseph H. Lewis; Ninth Kentucky, Col. Thomas H. Hunt. The first formal announcement of the Brigade was in General Order No. 51, October 1861, by Gen. Albert Sidney Johnston. It was commanded in whole or in part at different times: Brig.-Generals Simon B. Buckner, John C. Breckinridge, William Preston, Roger W. Hanson, Ben Hardin Helm and Joseph H. Lewis. It was complimented by the Generals Albert Sidney Johnston, P.G.T. Beauregard, Braxton Bragg, Joseph Johnston and John B. Hood.

The Orphan Brigade fought in every State east of the Mississippi and in front of almost every State capital in the South; opened many of the battles in which it was engaged, and often covered the retreats. No soldiers were better drilled; they won every prize in the army drills, the most notable being the brigade drill at Tullahoma, Tenn., in May, 1863.

In battle the Orphan Brigade "always charged and captured the enemy's stronghold," but the loss was great. At Shiloh it lost 844 out of 2401; Murfreesboro, 431 out of 812; at Chickamauga 471 out of a total of 1312. Prof. Shaler in his *Scribner's* article states that the one hundred days battle from Dalton to Atlanta, and on to the surrender, surpasses all records:

"The moral and physical patience exhibited being without a parallel in ancient or modern history. The Orphan Brigade left Dalton, May 7, 1864, with 1140 men, reached Atlanta (one hundred days later) with 240; they had received more than 2,000 wounds, there being only forty men in the entire command free from a bullet mark."

The military career of the Brigade closed with its disbandment Saturday, May 6, 1865, at Washington, Ga. Returning home to Kentucky, the Orphan Brigade took high rank in the walks of peace. It has furnished one Governor, three United States Senators, three Judges of the Court of Appeals, seven Congressmen, and many have held minor offices Auditor of State, State Superintendent of Education, Mayors, Sheriffs, Legislators, etc. A great many have become educators and ministers of the gospel – at one re-union a soldier called out the names of five of his regiment who were preachers.

The first reunion was held at Blue Lick Springs, 1882. Other reunions have been: Lexington, 1883; Elizabethtown, 1884; Glasgow, 1885; Cynthiana, 1886; Bardstown, 1887; Frankfort, 1888; Louisville, 1889; Lawrenceburg, 1890; Owensboro, 1891; Paris, 1892; Versailles, 1893; Russellville. 1894; Bowling Green, 1895; Nashville, Tennessee, 1896.

www.ingramcontent.com/pod-product-compliance
Lightning Source LLC
Chambersburg PA
CBHW071548040426
42452CB00008B/1106